ARE YOU *Listening?*

HEARING HIS WORD, DOING HIS WILL

GLORIA COPELAND

Harrison House
Tulsa, Oklahoma

Are You Listening?
Hearing His Word, Doing His Will
ISBN 157794-195-0   30-0553

07 06 05 04 03 02 01 00   10 9 8 7 6 5 4 3 2 1

Copyright © 2000 by Gloria Copeland
Kenneth Copeland Ministries
Fort Worth, Texas 76192-0001

Published by Harrison House, Inc.
P.O. Box 35035
Tulsa, Oklahoma 74153

CONTENTS

We are so blessed to be alive in this hour when all things are coming to fullness. The Church of the Lord Jesus Christ is beginning to possess the full abundance of blessings God always desired His people to enjoy.

Think about it—Jesus is coming soon, and every Bible promise we've ever believed has to come into manifestation between now and the moment He returns! All of God's will must be fulfilled now. Not one prayer spoken in faith according to the Word can go unanswered.

You and I were born for this hour. There has never been an hour like this before. The Church of Jesus Christ—His Body—has never been as full of the knowledge and presence of Him as it is in this day. It is in this unique hour of mankind's history that God's dream for His family is finally coming to pass. All over the world, church buildings are full of people who are listening to anointed apostles, prophets, evangelists, pastors and teachers reveal to them how to live by faith, separate themselves unto the Lord and obey the Word of God.

The time is short. The Church must follow God's plans and purposes in these last days. God has to have a people for this hour who will both *hear* and *do* His Word, because that's how His will comes to pass in this earth.

This world we live in won't get any better. The Scriptures tell us that as the day of Jesus' return approaches, the world will grow darker and darker; it will become more and more confused and evil. But in the Church, God will shine His light brighter and brighter!

That's what I see happening today. I've never seen the Word of God come forth with such clarity. Even when I just study the Word for myself, it seems so much clearer and easier to grasp and so much more difficult to misunderstand.

As the day of Jesus' return approaches, revelation will continue to increase. God's people will receive more and more light from the Word of God, and an increasing number of believers will choose to walk according to the ways of God's kingdom. As these believers rely on the supernatural help of the Holy Spirit and daily fellowship with God in His Word and in prayer, they will become more and more independent of this world's system. They will learn to live free in the midst of spiritual darkness, well in the midst of sickness, peaceful in the midst of turmoil, kind in the midst of hatred, secure and safe in the midst of terror, prosperous in the midst of lack.

That is the *only* way to live in this hour! As long as we purpose to continually *hear* the Word and then to *do* what God says, our victory in this life is virtually assured! We have a written guarantee!

Sometimes it may look as if taking a step of obedience is to your disadvantage. But let me assure you, God loves you and has only your good in mind. God is good, and only good comes from Him. He will never take away from you but will only increase blessing in your life as you obey Him. You just need to take the step of faith and determine to do what He says, at any cost.

That's all God ever really asks of any of us. He just wants us to say, "Yes, Lord"—and then do what He's told us to do!

Gloria Copeland

CHAPTER 1

THREE WORDS
AWAY FROM
VICTORY

God is so good! His great desire for us is to be whole and complete—nothing missing, nothing broken. It's important to Him that we live in His blessings. And to help us succeed, God by His Spirit makes His wisdom—His way of doing things—simple enough for us to understand how to walk in freedom and victory. In fact, I can give you God's basic victory class in just three words: *Hear and do!*

Everything that includes victory in God centers around those three words. All the victory you and I have ever experienced in our lives, from the moment we were born again to the present, came about because we heard what God said in His Word and in our hearts and then did it.

HEARKENING TO GOD'S WORD

And it gets even simpler! Those three words *hear and do* can be summed up in just one Bible word: *Hearken.*

My definition of *hearken* is "to give heed to; to pay attention; TO HEAR WITH THE INTENT TO DO." You see, hearing just isn't enough. The only way God's Word will ever do you any

good is for you to live by what you hear. We have to be willing to make adjustments so that we act in agreement with what God says.

WALK IN GOD'S WISDOM

This concept of hearing and doing the Word is actually walking in God's wisdom. The Bible defines *the wisdom of God* as God's way of doing things. Proverbs 14:8 in the *Amplified* version says that godly wisdom is **"comprehensive insight into the ways and purposes of God."**

So when we hear and do, we are actually obeying God's command to *get* and then *live by* His wisdom (Proverbs 4:7). That divine wisdom first came out of God's mouth and is now recorded in the written Word. Today we can look in this divinely inspired Book that we call "the Bible" and find out exactly the right and the wrong way to act in every situation of life. It's all there in black and white.

You don't even have to wonder, *Could this really be the correct answer?* You just have to determine in yourself, *I believe the Word of God is inspired, supernatural, alive and powerful, and I will obey it completely.* When you receive the Word that way, it makes a change in your life and places you into the stream of God's wisdom and His victorious plan for your life.

ONE MESSAGE THROUGH THE AGES

The Lord has been talking to me about those three words *hear and do* for a while now. It started when I decided to read through the book of Jeremiah in my private devotion time.

As I read through Jeremiah, I saw in a fresh way how faithful God is and how He works. It struck me that God's message to

Israel through the prophet Jeremiah stayed basically the same over a span of about 40 years of ministry. Throughout that time, God said to Israel again and again, "Hearken to Me. Do what I say, and I'll be able to bless you. But if you don't obey Me, I *won't* be able to favor you, and you'll go into bondage."

Then I began to realize something a little clearer and deeper than I ever had before. Over and over throughout 6,000 years of Bible history, all God ever asked of *anyone* was to do what He said!

You can see it again and again in the Bible. When a person, a city or a nation chose to walk with God, they lived in victory. When they didn't, they lived in defeat. To the extent people heard what God said and then did it, they walked in freedom, victory and glory—and peace!

The Hebrew word for peace is *shalom*. It means "nothing missing, nothing broken," or *"to be whole."*[1] That kind of peace has always been God's plan for His covenant-keeping people.

Well, do you think that God's message is different for us today? No, it's still the same. In this world where the enemy prowls around seeking to steal, kill and destroy, there is no other liberty for us outside of the Word of God. We'll walk in victory when we do what God tells us to do.

That's all God asks of us. He never asks us to perform miracles. He just tells us to do whatever He says, and then *He* will do whatever it takes to keep us whole.

From the Garden of Eden all the way to this present day and hour, God has asked that one thing. He asked it of Adam and Eve, of the Old Testament prophets, of Israel, of the Church. From Genesis to Revelation, from one generation to the next, the crux

---

[1] W. E. Vine, *Vine's Expository Dictionary of Biblical Words* (Nashville: Thomas Nelson Publishers, 1985), p. 173.

of the entire Word of God is this divine message: *"Hearken* to what I say to you."

There was a reason that God constantly endeavored to teach His people to obey Him: He wanted them to live in victory. So all through the Bible, you'll find Him talking to His people, sending them prophets as witnesses of Himself and revealing His good plan for them. God always did His best to cause Israel to hear what He was saying so they could obey and live free from bondage.

This one thing God asks. This one thing He should have—by all rights—because He is God: that His people would do what He says.

THE BOTTOM LINE

That's really the bottom line to everything. It's the key to any situation we face. It's the way we get healed. It's the way we stay delivered. It's the way we prosper in life. There is sure action from heaven when we *hear* from God and then *do* what we hear.

Because those three words *hear and do* are so important, we may think, *Those people God was talking to in the Bible should have wanted victory enough to obey Him!*

But the same sad situation exists today. People flip through television channels listening to one preacher after another teach from the Word about walking in victory. Then those same people get up and go through the day without ever acting on what they just heard!

But God just keeps asking His people to hear and obey Him so He can be involved in their lives. He desires to increase them, to bless them, to multiply them and to do them good. God demanded that from His people in the Bible, and He has never changed! He still says to us today, "If you want to be blessed, do what I say!"

NOAH'S WILLINGNESS TO BE "UNREASONABLE"

Six thousand years of Bible history prove that those who walked with God walked in victory. At times there may have been just one righteous person in an entire generation. For instance, Noah was the only one in his generation who walked with God.

Noah knew how to hear from God. But one day God told him to do something outlandish. Noah had never even seen rain before, yet God told him to build an ark! You see, at that time the ground wasn't watered by rain falling from the sky. Genesis 2:6 says, **"There went up a mist from the earth, and watered the whole face of the ground."**

Well, what would have happened to Noah if he had responded differently to God's instructions to build an ark? He could have argued, "I've never even seen an ark before. Rain? We've never even seen rain! Flood? What does that mean? How could a flood be coming? Where would it come from?"

That kind of reasoning would have made perfect sense to all the people around Noah. They would have considered it completely reasonable for Noah to decide *not* to build an ark.

Think about what God asked Noah to do. It was a big project! It took Noah a long time to build that ark, and the entire time it looked as if there were no reason in the world for him to be doing it.

I'm sure the people thought Noah was a crazy, old man. They probably talked among themselves, saying, "What is that thing Noah is building? A boat? Why is he building a boat on dry land so far away from any water? That old man has always seemed strange. He's always talking about God. He doesn't talk or act like the rest of us. He's a weirdo! He preaches righteousness, of all things!"

But that's all natural reasoning, and natural reasoning can keep you out of the will of God. What is "reasonable" mostly represents what the *world* says is right and normal. But the world is messed up! Worldly people have no idea what God's perspective is on any given situation. Many times they even think *evil* is right and normal! That's because natural people live in darkness. Without God and His Word, there is no light.

God is light, and God is right. When you walk by faith, you will often look unreasonable to the people around you.

That's why God told Abraham to get away from his relatives and go somewhere else, away from all he had known before. God says the same thing to the New Testament Church: **"Wherefore come out from among them** [the unsaved], **and be ye separate, saith the Lord"** (2 Corinthians 6:17).

We have to make a choice in this life whether we will follow God's way to victory or the world's more "reasonable" way to defeat. Personally, I'm choosing God! Ken and I have lived in victory for more than 32 years. We have proven that doing God's Word makes us free—and we love being free!

YOUR PART IS DO-ABLE!

God's way may seem unreasonable to the natural mind, but it is never impossible. God doesn't tell you to do something you can't do. You can always do your part.

You can obey. You can get born again and filled with the Holy Ghost. You can tithe. You can walk in love. You can continually feed your spirit on the Word of God and learn to hear the Holy Spirit when He speaks to you. Everything God tells you to do is do-able. He does the impossible part. Luke 18:27 says, **"The things which are impossible with men are possible with God."**

All things are possible to Him and, through Him, all things become possible to you. As Mark 9:23 says, **"All things are possible to him that believeth."**

The Lord recently said to me, *If you'll hear Me, I'll hear you.* We can see that truth proven out through centuries of Bible history. If God's people would hear Him and obey (which was their part), God would hear their cry and help them when they were in need. That's *His* part!

STAY IN A POSITION TO HEAR

Hear and do. It sounds pretty easy, doesn't it? It is especially easy when we realize that God is never wrong and only tells us to do things that will bring blessing into our lives! He always deals with us for our own good because our good is what pleases Him. I know that, because the Bible says God takes pleasure in the prosperity of His people! **"Let them shout for joy, and be glad, that favour my righteous cause: yea, let them say continually, Let the Lord be magnified, which hath pleasure in the prosperity of his servant"** (Psalm 35:27).

On the other hand, if you're in any kind of bondage, God can't be pleased because He wants you to be free. So He makes His instructions simple. If you want to be free, find out what's in the Book and do it!

Although hearing and doing *is* a simple concept, it may seem difficult at times to stay in a position where you can hear. That's your part, and you *can* do it. But it takes discipline and diligent effort. You have to spend time fellowshiping with God in the Word and in prayer. You have to live a life that is conducive to hearing Him. You can't just live a cluttered-up, carnal life and expect to hear from heaven.

I'm determined to keep myself in a position to hear from the Holy Spirit at all times. I want to go on in my walk with God. I want to press that issue as diligently and as far as I can! I want to do everything in this life that God wants me to—from the basic way I run my everyday life to the way I answer His call to minister His Word.

It's that kind of commitment to stay faithful in simple, daily acts of obedience that causes God to manifest Himself in your life. As a minister, I know it doesn't work to say, "I'm going to please God in my preaching. But in my everyday life, I'll live like everyone else." No, it's a minister's everyday life of obedience that enables him to reveal the Word of God in the power of God. Without a godly life to back his preaching, his words are mere words.

So just make the decision: "I lay before the Lord everything in my life, from the least to the greatest. I want to live, think, talk and act like God wants me to. What *He* says is right is what *I* say is right. And I'll do what He tells me to do, in the Name of Jesus, to the best of my ability and with His help."

And what if the Holy Spirit tells you, *"Turn off that television set"*? Don't argue with Him and say, "Well, Lord, I don't watch anything that is bad." God may be telling you to turn off the television because you can't hear from Him with all that noise filling your home for hours at a time!

In our "noise generation," we're very seldom in a place where it's quiet. We have television. We have radios. We have CDs. We have videos. We have DVDs. And who knows what the next noisemaker will be?

All these different kinds of noise that surround us can distract and clutter up our minds. But when we are alone in the car without the radio on, or when we're out in the quiet of a forest, sitting under a tree, most of us can't sit there for five minutes without talking to God. When our minds get quiet, it's just natural for our spirits to want to communicate with God.

Well, that fellowship with God is what you want to cultivate. That's practicing the presence of Jesus. Just talk to Him all the time, and He'll talk back to you! Don't make Him struggle with you to get you to listen, or you'll soon become dull of hearing. Give Him opportunity to visit with you.

If you're serious about hearing from heaven, you need to shut out the noise of the world and do what Psalm 46:10 says: **"Be still, and know that I am God."** Just quiet your mind and begin to hold a conversation with God. Talk to Him, and then listen to what He says in your heart. It is easier for me to start that at the beginning of the day before my mind gets busy and preoccupied. Then practice maintaining a hearing heart as you go through your day by talking with the Lord. Worship Him. Thank Him. Honor Him. Listen to Him. Obey Him. You have been invited to **"come boldly unto the throne of grace"** (Hebrews 4:16). Accept His invitation!

As you spend time fellowshiping with God on a daily basis, you'll be abiding, vitally united with the Vine, Jesus Christ—He in you, His Word in you and you in Him (John 15:1, 7, AMP). When you remain in living contact with Jesus, hearing and obeying what He tells you to do, He promises that you can ask what you will, and it shall be done for you!

> **I am the True Vine, and My Father is the Vinedresser....**
> **If you live in Me [abide vitally united to Me] and My**
> **words remain in you and continue to live in your hearts,**
> **ask whatever you will, and it shall be done for you.**
>
> **(John 15:1, 7, AMP)**

THROW YOURSELF OVER ON GOD

You have the ability to stay in a position to hear God. You also have the authority to tear up the devil's works and plunder his house for God's kingdom. But to walk in victory in these areas, you have to be diligent about the things of God.

I'm telling you, walking in the dominion of God's kingdom is not a casual undertaking. Living a complacent lifestyle in which you obey only the convenient parts of the Word is not what causes heavenly breakthroughs. The only way you can live in victory is to be diligent about putting God and His Word first place in your life and to continually walk in obedience to the light that you have.

Now, you might receive a miracle every once in a while with that kind of casual lifestyle. But I'm talking about living in the supernatural provision of heaven on a daily basis while you're still in a natural body. You just can't do that without being diligent.

You see, there isn't any good middle ground here. Trying to keep one foot in the world and one foot in God's kingdom just spells defeat and confusion. A person like that is a lukewarm Christian, and Jesus said He will spew lukewarm Christians out of His mouth (Revelation 3:16)!

Why would Jesus say that about lukewarm Christians? Because if you are lukewarm, you have had the opportunity to be diligent and on fire for God, and you turned it down.

You have to disconnect from the world's system to really get hold of the ways of God's kingdom. Too many Christians try to combine the best of the world's system with the laws of the kingdom. So they don't develop themselves in either realm, and they end up doing nothing significant with their lives.

Don't let yourself fall into that trap. Get on over to where freedom is. Throw yourself on God! Say, "Lord, I'm going Your way or no way, no matter what." That's what faith is all about.

Back in the late '60s when Ken and I first began to walk by faith, we didn't really know what we were doing. We were acting beyond our knowledge because we didn't understand all we do now about God's ways. (Of course, there's still plenty left for us to learn!)

But we did understand this: We wanted to grow in the things of God! So we determined together to obey the Word, no matter what it told us to do. One day we came upon Romans 13:8, where God tells us to **"owe no man any thing, but to love one another."** The revelation of that scripture hit our hearts, and we made the decision to never borrow money again.

Truthfully, we thought that decision was our doom. At the time, there wasn't anyone preaching that you could live without debt. We thought our decision not to borrow money meant we would have to go without material things we needed, such as a good home or a new car. We had never heard of anyone paying cash for a house, nor had we considered even buying a car without debt.

Not only that, we were preparing for full-time ministry. How could we enter the ministry without borrowing money if we didn't have the things necessary to begin?

But the mercy of God helped us make that bold faith decision. Then the Holy Spirit taught us how to walk it out.

YOU CAN'T OUT-HONOR GOD

You see, it might seem like a big thing to say, "Lord, I'm throwing myself over on You. Even if it looks like I'll go without,

I'm never going to borrow another dime." But you can't honor God with your faith and obedience beyond what He can handle.

Kenneth and I didn't know the end result when we made that commitment not to borrow any more money. We just believed God wanted us to do it, so we did it. It was God's mercy that got us to that point, because we didn't have the revelation knowledge at that time to back that decision. It was in our hearts but not in our heads!

The desire to honor God's Word by getting out and staying out of debt dropped in our hearts, and we committed ourselves to doing it. Even if we had never prospered, we would have held true to that commitment just to honor God.

You see, you just can't out-honor God. In 1 Samuel 2:30, He promises, **"Them that honour me I will honour."** The more you honor God with your diligent obedience to His Word, the more He'll manifest Himself in your life.

DILIGENT COURAGE TO STEP OUT IN FAITH

That's why the Bible is so full of scriptures about diligence (Proverbs 10:4, 13:4, 22:29). God knows it requires diligence on our part in order to give Him the time and attention it takes to stay in that place where we can first hear Him and then have the courage to do what He says.

Ken has always been an exciting person to follow after, particularly in the early days of our ministry, because he has always been so courageous about doing whatever God has said to do. I mean, many times he would just leave the rest of us standing in the dust as he zoomed on ahead in faith!

When Ken received a word from God, he wouldn't even think about anything else. He'd just start proclaiming in faith the dream

God had placed in his heart, such as, "We're going on every available radio station!" The rest of us would just have to try to catch on to his coattail so we wouldn't be left behind!

Ken's diligence and faith in this area have brought this ministry to where it is today. If we had waited for me to decide what to do, I might still be trying to figure it out! I'd be thinking, *Well, how can we do that? How will we pay for it?*

But Ken just stands behind the pulpit and declares the great faith endeavors God has given him to accomplish. Just recently he got up on the platform and said, "We're going on television all over the world!" So here we go again—taking a leap of faith as we practice those three words of victory—HEAR AND DO!

Kenneth has always had the courage to make those faith decisions and then start putting them in motion. And I guarantee you, it wasn't always easy to do that. Great faith victories don't come without a lot of pressure from circumstances and from the strategies of the enemy.

Mark 4:35-41 gives an enlightening account of dealing with pressure. Jesus told the disciples, "Let's go to the other side of the Sea of Galilee" (v. 35). But on their way over, a terrible storm suddenly arose, threatening to sink their boat.

That was a high-pressure situation, and the disciples didn't do very well at first. Instead of focusing on the Greater One Who had said, "We're going to the other side," they chose to focus on what they heard, saw and felt. They let the pressure of the circumstances get them into fear.

Finally, they called on Jesus and brought His power on the scene. As soon as Jesus spoke words of faith, the storm was stilled, peace was restored and the boat sailed safely to the other side.

The disciples had to learn the same lesson that you do today: If you'll do what God tells you to do, He will manage the rest of it. He'll do the impossible part as you hear and do your possible part!

Kenneth and I have been walking this way now for most of our lives. In fact, we have lived by faith for more years than we have lived in unbelief! And I'm a witness today of the fact that the extent to which you diligently hear and do the Word is the extent to which the blessings of God will be able to manifest in your life. When you sell out to God, God sells out to you! When you hear Him, He hears you!

Prayer of Consecration

Lord, I set myself to hear and obey You. For anything I've let slip, I ask You to forgive me. I ask You, Lord, to bring it to me again if I've forgotten what it is. Give me another opportunity. I'll be quicker to hear and quicker to do than I've ever been before!

THINK ON THESE THINGS

*I can give you God's basic victory class
in just three words: Hear and do!*

*Over and over throughout 6,000 years of Bible history,
all God ever asked of anyone was to do what He said!*

*There is sure action from heaven when we
hear from God and then do what we hear.*

CHAPTER 2

A GENERATION
PREPARED FOR
THIS HOUR

G od has always wanted a people who would hear and do His Word. But never has it been so crucial for believers to do what God tells them to as it is in this end-time hour before Jesus returns.

ISRAEL: HOLINESS UNTO THE LORD

That truth hit my heart recently as I studied the book of Jeremiah and started seeing God's recurring message to hear and do. I read a scripture that opened up my understanding concerning what God is doing on the earth in these last days. He is preparing a generation for this final hour.

Go and cry in the ears of Jerusalem, saying, Thus says the Lord: I [earnestly] remember the kindness and devotion of your youth, your love after your betrothal [in Egypt] and marriage [at Sinai] when you followed Me in the wilderness, in a land not sown. Israel was holiness [something set apart from ordinary purposes, dedicated] to the Lord, the firstfruits of His harvest [of which no stranger was allowed to partake]; all who ate

of it [injuring Israel] offended and became guilty; evil came upon them, says the Lord.

(Jeremiah 2:2-3, AMP)

When I read these verses, something just went off in my heart as I realized the significance of that statement: Israel was holiness to the Lord.

In this passage of Scripture, God was talking about Israel's long sojourn with Him in the wilderness. The generation that grew up in the wilderness was consecrated or dedicated unto Him as the first fruits of His harvest. I had never before realized that God had to send the children of Israel to the wilderness to prepare for Himself a generation sanctified and made holy unto Him.

In Hebrew, the word translated *to be holy* also means "to sanctify"[1]; "to take out and separate unto God." According to *Vine's*, the word *sanctify* means "an act whereby, or a state wherein, people or things are set aside for…the worship of God [and]… treated with special care as a possession of God."[2]

Another word that means basically the same thing as sanctified is *devoted*. The tithe is a good example of something that is devoted to the Lord. God designed the tithe to be used by Him for His purposes. We separate the first fruits and the best of our increase from the rest of our finances and set them apart for Him.

Now, that word *devoted* can also mean "set apart for destruction" in some cases. Let's just stay with the example of your tithe. You may decide to keep the tithe, but you won't be able to use it for yourself. It's either devoted to the Lord, or it's devoted to destruction.

---

[1] W. E. Vine, *Vine's Expository Dictionary of Biblical Words* (Nashville: Thomas Nelson Publishers, 1985), p. 114.

[2] Ibid. p. 210.

As one preacher said, tithe money that isn't devoted to the Lord will just blow up in your pocket. You'll have to spend it on one crisis after the other until it's all used up. Right after the refrigerator needs repair, the car will break down. Or you will have unexpected medical bills—and on and on it goes.

Just like the tithe, you and I are devoted to the Lord. For instance, 1 Corinthians 3:16 says your body, the temple of the Holy Spirit, is holy. And just like withholding the tithe causes it to be devoted to destruction, if you don't keep your body the way you should by obeying God, it will begin to destruct.

The reason God has called us, as His sons and daughters, to live set-apart and sanctified lives is not because He wants to be a dictator. It's because He knows what is best for us. Each of us is a spirit being. We have a soul (mind, will and emotions) and we live in a body. Being devoted to God involves all three. That simply means that we obey God in everything He tells us to do—we live for Him and refuse to participate in the world's ungodliness.

As you spend time in prayer and in God's Word, your spirit relays to your soul what the Spirit of God is saying to you. According to Hebrews 4:12, the Word of God divides between the soul and the spirit. It will distinguish within you between what is coming from your mind and what is coming from your spirit. Then it's up to you to be obedient and walk holy (separated) in your body.

THE CONSEQUENCES OF UNBELIEF

Because of disobedience, God sent the children of Israel into the wilderness to prepare for Himself another generation of people who would do what He said. This new generation did not include anyone over 20 years of age. God plainly told the older generation,

"You're not coming out; you'll die in the wilderness. You'll never see the Promised Land because of your unbelief and your sin" (Numbers 14:29-30, author's paraphrase).

That generation had heard the Word of God, but they didn't mix faith with it (Hebrews 4:2). They didn't believe what they had heard, and they wouldn't hearken to what God was telling them to do through Moses to possess the land He had given them.

God said, "Go in and possess the land and I'll be with you." They said, "No, we can't go take that land. Those Canaanites are too big for us to fight. They have big walls over there. It's a good place, all right, and it has a lot of wonderful things in it—but there are giants in that land! We're just a bunch of grasshoppers in comparison. We can't fight them!" (Numbers 13:26-29, 31-33, author's paraphrase).

So the people refused to go up to possess the land. Instead, they began to murmur, saying, "Why do we have to die? We would have been better off in Egypt!" (Numbers 14:3). They forgot what Egypt was like. They forgot how hard it was to make bricks without straw. They forgot the cruel taskmasters. They would not obey.

Finally, they pushed God one step too far. He told them, "You've gone too far this time. You have tempted Me 10 times, and that's one time too many. You are going to die right here in this wilderness, and the only ones coming out again are Joshua and Caleb and those under 20 years old" (See Numbers 14:22-23, 29-30, author's paraphrase).

Now, what if God had brought this generation of unbelievers out of the wilderness? What if He had left them at the border of the Promised Land with all those Canaanites and the other "-ites" surrounding them? The Israelites would have been destroyed, because they were not in faith and they did not believe the prophet God had sent them.

The Scripture says, **"Believe in the Lord your God, so shall ye be established; believe his prophets, so shall ye prosper"** (2 Chronicles 20:20). But the Israelites wouldn't believe Moses. They wouldn't believe Joshua and Caleb, either. Instead, they believed the evil report of unbelief. Unbelief is an evil report!

The people were out of God's will, so they couldn't go out against the enemy and be successful because of disobedience. God no longer had legal ground to take their part and defeat their enemies for them. So He had no choice; He left them in the wilderness until all the disobedient, rebellious people died. It wasn't God who killed those people; they just died in the desert because of their own contrariness!

Unbelief is dangerous, isn't it? That older generation wouldn't walk by faith. They wouldn't go in and possess their Promised Land. So they wandered in the wilderness for the rest of their days on this earth—because they would not hear and do what God had said to them.

THE YOUNGER GENERATION— SET APART FOR GOD'S PURPOSES

Meanwhile, the younger generation grew up in the wilderness knowing nothing but God. Out there, God supernaturally fed them. God took care of them. God gave them light by night and a cloud to guide them by day.

These young people didn't grow up among the heathen, exposed to their evil practices and foreign gods. Instead, they grew up eating manna from heaven every day! Think about that.

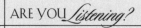

They saw the power of God in manifestation every time they ate a meal!

Growing up in the wilderness, they never saw lack. Every day of their lives, they saw that their shoes didn't wear out. Their clothes didn't wear out. They grew up knowing only God's ways and His supernatural provision.

The younger generation was also raised hearing about God all the time. They heard their parents talking about the signs and wonders that God had performed to deliver them out of Egypt. They heard about how great God is and how He had parted the Red Sea. I mean, those older Israelites may have been an unbelieving bunch, but it's just natural to sit around the campfire at night and talk about memories as spectacular as these were.

I can just hear those older Israelites talking to each other: "Do you remember the old days, Elizabeth, when God made both sides of that sea stand up? They stood right up, and we walked across on dry ground! How did that happen, Liz?"

"I don't know, Zedekiah—I just know we did it!"

The children also heard their parents talk about how they failed to obey God. How do I know the parents talked about that? Listen, people don't make serious mistakes that cost them everything in life and then never talk about it! They knew that rebellion against God's Word put them in the wilderness.

The children probably heard their parents asking themselves, "Why didn't we go over into the Promised Land when God told us to? Why didn't we obey God? Look at where our unbelief and rebellion have gotten us!

"We've been in this lousy wilderness for 35 years now! We could have been in the Promised Land all this time. Why didn't we listen to Joshua and Caleb? Now we'll never see the Promised

Land. I wish we had been obedient. If I had it to do over again, I'd obey God!"

As the children listened to their parents, the importance of hearing and doing sank deeply in their hearts. So, little by little, through their years of wilderness life, these young people became a generation separated unto God—the generation God prepared to obey Him and to go inherit the Promised Land.

You see, God wasn't going to quit just because the entire older generation (except for Joshua and Caleb) failed to obey Him. One way or another, He would find a way to keep His covenant with Abraham and his seed.

God had to raise up a people who would do what He said. He needed a people who would enter into the rest of faith, believing His promise that He would go with them and give them the Promised Land, despite the heavy odds that were against them in the natural.

It was obvious that the generation under Moses were not to be that people because they would not hearken unto God. So God raised up a "Joshua generation"—a people who were willing to believe what He said and follow Joshua into the Promised Land to possess it.

JOSHUA AND CALEB'S SPIRIT OF FAITH

Joshua and Caleb were the only two faithful spies of the 12 who had spied out the land. These two men believed what God had told them. They told the people, "God is for us—we can take the land! Those giants will be nothing before us with God on our side!" (Numbers 14:8-9).

So over the next 40 years, these two men of valor watched every one of their contemporaries—all the men they had fought battles with—die in the wilderness, while they continued to stay strong.

Now, Joshua and Caleb could have become bitter. They could have said, "God, we did everything we knew to do. But all those other jerks got into disobedience, and now here we are, wandering around in the wilderness with them year after year!"

But these two faith giants didn't do that. They just kept holding on to God's promise for those 40 long years. Finally, they were left with a completely new generation. By the time God passed the torch of leadership from Moses to Joshua, the younger man had a people to work with who would obey what God said.

This generation had a different spirit about them. They had grown up free from the evil practices of the world. They were willing to do what Joshua told them to do—unlike their fathers, who would sometimes follow Moses and more often rebel.

Meanwhile, God hadn't forgotten what He had told Joshua and Caleb. You see, God is very exact. Many years earlier He had told the men, because of their willingness to obey Him, "You two are going to inherit the land," and His word still held true. God never forgets obedience and loyalty.

So five years into the campaign to take the Promised Land, Caleb came to Joshua and said, "I'm 85 years old now, but I'm just as strong today as I was when I went to spy out the land 45 years ago. Give me that mountain, Joshua. God gave it to me—it's mine!" (Joshua 14:7-12).

Caleb had heard a word from the Lord, and for 45 years he held on to that word. Through 40 years of hearing murmuring and complaining and all kinds of unbelief, Caleb believed God!

Then he did exactly what God had told him to do. He took by conquest what God had promised. Caleb possessed his promised mountain! Joshua 14:14 says Caleb received his inheritance **"because that he wholly followed the Lord God of Israel."** That is exactly how to receive your inheritance from God!

WE ARE A SET-APART GENERATION

God called the generation of Israel that finally possessed the Promised Land "holiness unto Him." I had never seen it exactly like that before. God had to have a generation set apart from ordinary purposes and dedicated to Him for His purposes—the first fruits of His harvest.

When I shared this revelation with Kenneth, he said, "Well, you know, Gloria, you and I are like that generation of Israelites. We've been separated from the world for more than 32 years!"

I started thinking about it, and that's absolutely the truth. For more than three decades, Ken and I have been learning to obey God both in the written Word and in what He tells us to do individually. God has been in the process of renewing our minds and transforming our lives by teaching us His way of doing things.

The same is true for every other Christian who has committed himself to hearing and doing the Word. We have all been separated from the world as holiness unto God for as long as we have endeavored to obey Him. God has been teaching us His Word, training us to live like He lives, to believe what He says, to say what He says, to act like He says we should act and to minister to people by His Spirit.

We've already seen that God calls the children of Israel the first fruits of His harvest in Jeremiah 2:3. But in the book of James, the Bible also calls us a kind of first fruits:

> And it was of His own [free] will that He gave us
> birth [as sons] by [His] Word of Truth, so that we
> should be a kind of firstfruits of His creatures [a sample
> of what He created to be consecrated to Himself].
>
> (James 1:18, AMP)

Just as the children of Israel were separated unto God out there in the wilderness, we have been separated unto God for this hour. God had to have a people right now who would separate themselves from the world's ways and commit themselves to obey Him. He had to raise up a generation of Word people—believers separated unto His Word to hear and do what it says. We are a kind of first fruits, separated out from the world unto Him and for His purposes. His plan must be fulfilled. God has "appointed times." He is never late!

MORE REVELATION—ACCELERATED GROWTH

Did you know that there hasn't always been a widespread group of Word people? Certainly not to the degree that there is today. When Ken and I started listening to Kenneth Hagin and learning how to walk by faith more than 32 years ago, there were very few churches that actually preached the message of living by faith.

I'm talking about the kind of lifestyle in which you don't just talk about the Word of God; you live it. You don't just act like a faith person on Sunday. You depend on what God has already said to get your needs met. You operate by God's promises the way Abraham did.

When you get in trouble, you go to the Word. To learn how to stay out of trouble, you go to the Word. To find out how to conduct your life or to obtain the finances to achieve your dream, you go to the Word. In short, God and His Word are always first place in your life!

Now, I'm not saying there weren't any good churches or pastors back then. But hardly anyone was teaching people how to live that kind of bold lifestyle of faith.

In fact, the Lord told Ken in those early years of ministry, *Go hold meetings in neutral places. Let the people come to you. Don't go to the churches.* The ministers would actually sit on the platform and shake their heads in disapproval, while Ken stood in the pulpit preaching faith.

God told Ken to go to neutral venues, because the people hearing the Word have to receive the Word. If it's preached and not received, it doesn't profit. It has to be mixed with faith. There is no profit in preaching the Word of faith in a church where the people have too much unbelief and religious tradition cluttering their hearts to receive the message!

As Charles Capps says, "The Bible is so simple, you have to have help to misunderstand it." Unfortunately, there has been a lot of help!

THEN AND NOW

In the late '60s, Kenneth Hagin began holding 10-day seminars every three months in Tulsa, where his ministry is based. (In those days, a minister had to have long meetings. It took at least a week or two for a minister to get over the resistance of religious tradition and unbelief. Then after the people settled down and began to hear what he had to say, he could have a good three-day meeting!)

We were living in Tulsa at the time Ken was attending Oral Roberts University, and we started going to these 10-day meetings. Kenneth Hagin would cover subjects we had never heard before, such as spirit, soul and body.

Ken and I became consumed with the desire to learn more about the Word. We went to every meeting, never missing a service. We took our little children; we ventured out on icy streets. We did whatever it took to hear the Word of God.

Do you know how many people cared enough about the Word of God to come to those meetings back then? The building held about 150 people. I don't remember it ever being overfilled. In those little meetings, we knew just about everybody by name.

People just didn't know much about the Word in those days. I'm telling you, if you haven't been in this walk of faith as long as I have, you just don't realize how far the Body of Christ has come!

The situation is completely different today. Thousands of people travel every year to the Hagin Campmeeting in Tulsa and other faith conventions around the country. And when Ken and I travel through scores of little towns on cross-country motorcycle trips, it seems as if there is a Word church in every one of them. We can usually identify them by their names—Living Word Church, Victory Fellowship, Word of Faith Church, Faith Christian Center, etc. God is establishing a witness of His Word in towns all across America and the world!

And in every city, the churches that are preaching the Word of God—how to hear it, act on it, live by it—are the ones growing big in this day. Check it out—the mega-churches you read about even in secular publications are mostly Holy Ghost-filled Word churches. For the most part, they are also the ministries remaining on television.

Why? Because these ministries walk by faith and not by sight! God has raised up another generation of people who will let Him have His way.

We are that people. When God tells us to do something, we're ready to obey, no matter how far-out it looks or how big the giants are. We believe God can do anything that He says He can. We even believe He can use us to do it! (Believing that last part sometimes takes more faith than anything else!)

GOD LOOKS FOR HEARERS AND DOERS OF THE WORD

James goes on to tell us what it takes to be a part of the first fruits God desires us to be:

It was of His own [free] will that He gave us birth [as sons] by [His] Word of Truth, so that we should be a kind of firstfruits of His creatures [a sample of what He created to be consecrated to Himself]. Understand [this], my beloved brethren. Let every man be quick to hear [a ready listener], slow to speak, slow to take offense and to get angry.

For man's anger does not promote the righteousness God [wishes and requires]. So get rid of all uncleanness and the rampant outgrowth of wickedness, and in a humble (gentle, modest) spirit receive and welcome the Word which implanted and rooted [in your hearts] contains the power to save your souls.

But be doers of the Word [obey the message], and not merely listeners to it, betraying yourselves [into deception by reasoning contrary to the Truth]. For if anyone only listens to the Word without obeying it and

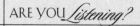
being a doer of it, he is like a man who looks carefully at his [own] natural face in a mirror;

For he thoughtfully observes himself, and then goes off and promptly forgets what he was like. But he who looks carefully into the faultless law, the [law] of liberty, and is faithful to it and perseveres in looking into it, being not a heedless listener who forgets but an active doer [who obeys], he shall be blessed in his doing (his life of obedience).

(James 1:18-25, AMP)

Hear and do. There's that same key again. As over the years many of us have heard and obeyed the Word of God, God has separated us unto Himself and made us a nation within a nation. We think God's higher thoughts and we live in God's higher ways (Isaiah 55:6-12).

God had to have a people for this hour who would hear His Word and obey it. He had to have a people who, like Moses and Joshua, at His Word would stretch forth their rod over an impassable sea or put their feet into a rushing river, all the while believing that somehow He would make a way for them. God simply will not operate on this earth without a people who will hear and do.

Ken and I have built our lives on that basic principle of obedience for more than three decades. Way back then, we determined that whatever the Word told us to do, we would be diligent to do it.

SEPARATED BY THE WORD OF TRUTH

Look at what Jesus said in His prayer to the Father:

I have given them thy word; and the world hath
hated them, because they are not of the world, even as
I am not of the world. I pray not that thou shouldest
take them out of the world, but that thou shouldest
keep them from the evil. They are not of the world,
even as I am not of the world. Sanctify them through
thy truth: thy word is truth.

(John 17:14-17)

Jesus prayed, "Sanctify them, Father. Purify, consecrate, separate them for Yourself. Make them holy by truth. Your Word is truth."

We're not of this kingdom down here on the earth. We're of the kingdom of God. The Word of God has entered our hearts and sanctified or separated us from the world so that we would hear the truth and act on it in our everyday lives.

I wouldn't trade being a doer of the Word for anything else in the world! There is no other way to separate yourself unto God, except by the truth of God's Word.

Now, there are different degrees of separation, but a life that is set apart unto God is available to all of us. Those of us who have been living this life of faith for a long time should be further along than someone who started last year. However, many who only recently began to live by faith are catching up fast! You can grow fast if you dedicate yourself to the challenge.

You see, even though you may be new to this walk of faith, I'm convinced of this: Those who are coming into the kingdom of God now are learning and gaining spiritual maturity much faster than 20 or 30 years ago.

Revelation of the Word is stronger now than it's ever been. It's the same revelation, but it's easier to get hold of than it was

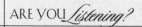

back then. Today we have opportunities that weren't available 30 years ago. We have television. We have video. We have good Bible-believing churches. We have Bible schools that teach how to live by faith.

There was no Bible school like that when Ken and I entered the ministry. We had to make our own Bible school by studying the Bible, reading books, listening to tapes and attending meetings. Now there are good Bible schools all over the world, teaching this message of faith.

I'm telling you, we are a generation prepared for this hour! We're training for whatever is going to happen between now and the time Jesus returns. We've been separated by the Word of God. We believe this Word. We don't care if the whole world says it's not true. We don't care what they say or think about us. We're determined to honor God's Word and do what He tells us to do. We're taking dominion in the Name of the Lord and seeing this final harvest through!

THE GOAL: UNITY OF THE FAITH

We just need to cut out the fluff, keep growing and keep our focus in the right place—on the Lord. As we keep putting God first in everything and doing what He tells us to do, we will eventually come into the unity of faith. So it's up to us. You do your part, and I'll do mine. Then in unity we will get the job done at any cost, in the Name of Jesus!

Let's go back and look at Jesus' prayer in John 17 in *The Amplified Bible:*

> **Just as You sent Me into the world, I also have sent them into the world. And so for their sake and on their**

behalf I sanctify (dedicate, consecrate) Myself, that they also may be sanctified (dedicated, consecrated, made holy) in the Truth....

I have given to them the glory and honor which You have given Me, that they may be one [even] as We are one: I in them and You in Me, in order that they may become one and perfectly united, that the world may know and [definitely] recognize that You sent me and that You have loved them [even] as You have loved me.

(vv. 18-19, 22-23)

The world as a whole has never yet been shown the power in that kind of unity within the Body of Christ. For Jesus' prayer to be answered, the world will have to see the Church operating in the power and the glory of God. And the Church can't come to that place of power and glory without hearing and doing what God says in His Word.

WE CAN DO IT!

But we can do it. We've been trained to do it! Just as God trained and set apart that generation of Israelites to take the Promised Land, He has been preparing in us a generation of separated Word people to fulfill His purposes in this final hour. He has taught us how to be people who will believe the Word of God and then do it.

We can be quick to obey God and quick to make adjust-ments. We can live separated unto God. We can be the first fruits that God desires to have for this hour.

God will keep His Word. Every word that has come out of His mouth, every appointed time He has spoken, will come to pass.

The baby Jesus was not one day late. Salvation was not one day late. It was an appointed time, and God had everything in place. Joseph, Mary and John the Baptist were ready to do their parts. The prayers of Anna and others had prepared the way for the appointed time. God had everything ready.

God is never late, He is never weak and He's never behind. Whatever He says, He *will* do.

God is also quite a maneuverer of people. He always manages to find enough obedient people to keep His timetable. Sometimes He will even come in person to talk to someone in order to get him or her on His track. But one way or another, even if He has to go to the back side of the desert, God will find somebody who will hear and do so that His Word is fulfilled.

The decision you have to make is this: "Am I going to be one of those somebodies? Am I going to be one of the set-apart generation, living by faith, separated from the world's ways by the Word of God?"

YOU ARE A DEVOTED TREASURE UNTO THE LORD

If you answer those questions with a resounding "Yes!" then begin to see yourself as devoted unto the Lord. Remember what Jeremiah 2:3 says about Israel, the first fruits of the Lord's harvest: **"[No stranger was allowed to partake]; all who ate of it [injuring Israel] offended and became guilty; evil came upon them, says the Lord"** (AMP).

In other words, you don't mess with God's separated people! You either join them or leave them alone.

For instance, people couldn't just go up to the Ark of the Covenant and examine it out of curiosity. If they did, it was fatal. That actually happened to some. Why? Because the Ark was devoted to the Lord. It had the presence of God in it. It had to be approached appropriately and with great precaution.

In the same way, you don't mess with the tithe. It's God's money. You don't just go do anything you want to do with God's money. You find out what God wants, and then you do that. Why? Because it's devoted. It belongs to God.

You belong to God. You are devoted as well. You have been set apart for His use. Ephesians 1:4 says you are holy before God in love. You can't live like other people. Whatever God tells you to do, you must do. You're His.

In Exodus 19:5-6, God talked about His desire for a holy, obedient people—a treasure devoted unto Him:

> **Now therefore, if ye will obey my voice indeed, and keep my covenant, then ye shall be a peculiar treasure unto me above all people: for all the earth is mine: And ye shall be unto me a kingdom of priests, and an holy nation.**

That's all God has ever wanted—a people He could work with who would faithfully hear and do. That's what He wants in you.

THE JOSHUA GENERATION

Let's look back again at "the Joshua generation" and the man of God who led them into the Promised Land. Studying some things about Joshua's life can help inspire us to become a part of today's "Jesus generation."

You never see a negative thing written about Joshua. Now, Moses made some mistakes. He let his temper get the best of

him, and it cost him the opportunity to enter the Promised Land. But not so with Joshua.

Joshua is the perfect pattern of Jesus, the One for Whom he was the type. In fact, *Jesus* and *Joshua* are the same name in different languages. The account of Joshua leading the children of Israel into the Promised Land is also a pattern of what is to happen in this generation before the return of Jesus Christ. As with the Joshua generation, we, too, will possess our promised land—the fullness of our inheritance in Christ.

So what made Joshua such an outstanding leader of God's people? For one thing, Joshua had experienced God's glory. He went up on Mount Sinai (which was covered with God's glory) as Moses' attendant when Moses separated himself from the people and stayed up on the mountain in the presence of God for 40 days (Exodus 24:13-18). The Bible also says in Exodus 33:10-11 that Joshua was with Moses when God's glory filled the tabernacle.

Then in Numbers 27:18, it says that Joshua was **"a man in whom is the spirit."** Joshua had the Spirit of God on him. He had been with Moses in the glory, and God was getting him ready to take Moses' place.

So God instructed Moses:

> **Take thee Joshua the son of Nun, a man in whom is the spirit, and lay thine hand upon him; And set him before Eleazar the priest, and before all the congregation; and give him a charge in their sight. And thou shalt put some of thine honour upon him, that all the congregation of the children of Israel may be obedient.**
>
> **(Numbers 27:18-20)**

Joshua had a good report with God. He was full of the Spirit. He was faithful. He had an anointing and, for the most part, the children of Israel hearkened unto him (Deuteronomy 34:9).

TAKE COURAGE—GOD WILL NEVER FORSAKE YOU!

Look at what God said to Joshua after Moses died:

> **Moses my servant is dead; now therefore arise, go over this Jordan, thou, and all this people, unto the land which I do give to them, even to the children of Israel.**
>
> **(Joshua 1:2)**

Joshua had been close to Moses as his faithful attendant. He probably had a tendency to feel a little depressed when his leader disappeared off the face of the earth. But here, God basically says to Joshua, "Get over it. You have a job to do here."

Then the Lord goes on to encourage Joshua:

> **There shall not any man be able to stand before thee all the days of thy life: as I was with Moses, so I will be with thee: I will not fail thee, nor forsake thee.**
>
> **(Joshua 1:5)**

As the Jesus generation, we have a similar promise to hold on to in Hebrews 13:5. *The Amplified Bible* says it this way:

> **He [God] Himself has said, I will not in any way fail you nor give you up nor leave you without support. [I will] not, [I will] not, [I will] not in any degree leave you helpless nor forsake nor let [you] down (relax My hold on you)! [Assuredly not!].**

That verse is mine! God will not fail me. He will not forsake me. He will not let me down. I have to hold on to that truth in times of pressure. Joshua had an opportunity to do that too. That's why God told him, **"Be strong and of a good courage"** (Joshua 1:6).

Sometimes it takes courage to obey the Word of God, especially when everything in sight says, "It's not going to work. You're doomed!" You have to just focus on the words of your Heavenly Father, Who says to you, "I will not fail you nor forsake you. Be strong and let your heart take courage to do what I tell you to do."

THE BLESSINGS OF DOING THE WORD

Then God tells Joshua, **"Turn not from it [God's Word] to the right hand or to the left"** (Joshua 1:7). Here are the results of obeying that command: **"That thou mayest prosper whithersoever thou goest."** Having the courage to act on the Word has great benefits—it causes you to prosper!

God repeats that same principle again in Joshua 1:8:

> **This book of the law shall not depart out of thy mouth; but thou shalt meditate therein day and night, that thou mayest observe to do according to all that is written therein: for then thou shalt make thy way prosperous, and then thou shalt have good success.**

God's message to Joshua was "Keep My Word in your mouth. Meditate on it, get it in your heart—and then do it. That's how you will prosper."

When you hear and do, you make your way prosperous. You don't have to worry about it. You don't even have to really ask

God to help you to prosper. Your obedience just naturally paves the way to success!

As soon as God finished talking to him, Joshua commanded the officers under him to follow the Lord's instructions (Joshua 1:10-15). Throughout his life, Joshua did whatever he was told. In fact, Joshua 11:15 says that Joshua **"left nothing undone of all that the Lord commanded Moses."**

Joshua is an inspiration. He was faithful. He was courageous. He was well trained. You couldn't shake him. He never stopped until he took all the land that the Lord had commanded him.

Well, we are the Jesus generation. We're going to be like Joshua. We won't leave any work undone that God has called us to do. We'll take all the territory that He tells us to take and win all the lost souls that He tells us to win. We're an obedient generation. We don't just talk—we hear and do!

Now let's look at the results of the Israelites' obedience to possess the Promised Land:

> **And the Lord gave unto Israel all the land which he sware to give unto their fathers; and they possessed it, and dwelt therein. And the Lord gave them rest round about, according to all that he sware unto their fathers: and there stood not a man of all their enemies before them; the Lord delivered all their enemies into their hand. There failed not aught of any good thing which the Lord had spoken unto the house of Israel; all came to pass.**
>
> **(Joshua 21:43-45)**

Everything God had promised Israel came to pass. The people possessed all the Promised Land because God finally had a leader and a people who would work together and do what He said. They conquered enemies stronger than they were; they inherited houses they didn't build; they received rain for one good harvest after another. Just as Joshua left nothing undone, so God left nothing undone in the fulfilling of His promises.

Now, God's promises would have come to pass for Moses' generation if they had obeyed Him. But they refused to hear and do, forfeiting their right to their reward.

You know, if you will plant this message deeply in your heart, it will save you a lot of heartache and wasted time. You have to determine, *I'm going to be quick to hear and quick to obey. I'm going to walk by faith!*

And remember—every time God asks you to do something, He backs you up with His anointing and His power. He doesn't intend for you to be out there trying to do what He tells you to all on your own. He wants you to do what you are told and then let Him do the impossible.

THE JESUS GENERATION

Joshua was one man with the Spirit of God on him. His obedience caused Israel to inherit all the great promises God had given them. Even after Joshua's death, the elders of that generation continued to walk with God, hearing and obeying His commands.

That's the picture of the Joshua generation. And we're the picture of the Jesus generation! We are first fruits unto Him, separated by the Word of God unto Him for this hour. God has never had a generation to work with like this one. But we're near the end of this age, and He has to have it now. We're right on time!

So many new ways are available to preach the gospel. We're the first generation to have television, the Internet, satellites, airplanes, videotapes, audiotapes and radio. There have never been so many books abounding full of God's truth.

Of course, all these avenues of communication are high-dollar items. A minister can't go on television and spend just a little bit of money; he has to spend millions of dollars every month.

That's why Satan's worst nightmare is a generation of believers who know the Word of God, walk by faith, walk in the ways of God and will do what they're told. And this generation is it!

We have been separated to walk by faith and not by sight, to speak faith words, to talk to mountains and see them removed, to allow God to perform miracles in our lives.

We have courage through the spirit of faith, just as our father Abraham had. He believed and he spoke, and he wasn't moved by anything, including his wife's and his own aged bodies. He was fully persuaded that God was able to keep His promise, and that's exactly what God did (Romans 4:16-21)!

The Spirit of God is in us. The spirit of faith is in us. We are strong and we are able because God is in us, and He makes us able!

We may be the last generation before Jesus returns, but we are a ready generation. We just need to do some fine-tuning and exercise more diligence in what we're doing. We must live unto God and give Him first place.

Be a part of the prepared generation. Whatever God tells you to do, whether it's spending more time in prayer and in the Word or making some other change in your life, take action on it. Follow through with it. You never know where that next step of obedience will take you, but you know it's God's best. Let God be God, and go take your promised land!

Prayer of Consecration

Lord, thank You for letting me be a part of this end-time Word generation. I'll stand strong. I'll believe big. I'll resist all the temptations the devil has to offer. I'll walk in the Word of God and be faithful to hear and do what You tell me to. My heart's desire is that at the end of my life, it will be said of me what was said of Joshua—that I left nothing undone that You told me to do!

THINK ON THESE THINGS

*God simply will not operate on this earth
without a people who will hear and do.*

*There is no other way to separate yourself
unto God, except by the truth of God's Word.*

*God is never late, He is never weak and
He's never behind. Whatever He says, He will do.*

*Having the courage to act on the Word
has great benefits—it causes you to prosper!*

*We're the picture of the Jesus generation! We are first fruits unto
Him, separated by the Word of God unto Him for this hour.*

*Satan's worst nightmare is a generation of believers
who know the Word of God, walk by faith, walk in
the ways of God and will do what they're told.*

You can grow fast if you dedicate yourself to the challenge.

CHAPTER 3

MAN'S FIRST
FAILURE TO
HEAR AND DO

From the beginning, God has had one major problem crop up again and again: people who refuse to hear and obey. Let's go back to the beginning and look at man's first failure to hear God's words and do them.

One thing I want you to see in this study is solid proof that God is good. It becomes obvious that His desire for man from the very beginning was to bless and prosper us beyond anything our minds can imagine.

BEFORE THE FALL

Adam and Eve, the first man and woman whom God created, were also the first man and woman who failed to hearken to God's Word. The account of this first act of disobedience is found in the book of Genesis.

In Genesis 2:7, we find that God breathed Himself into Adam and gave him life. Adam was created righteous, without sin. He was right with God. He didn't have an evil nature.

Then God said, **"It is not good that the man should be alone; I will make him an help meet for him"** (Genesis 2:18).

Oh, oh! Here is something in the Garden that isn't good! It isn't good for man to be alone!

So what did God do? He fixed the problem! He made Adam a wife to match him—a good wife who, just like him, possessed a nature devoid of all evil. He made them like Himself.

> **And God said, Let us make man in our image, after our likeness: and let them have dominion over the fish of the sea, and over the fowl of the air, and over the cattle, and over all the earth, and over every creeping thing that creepeth upon the earth.**
>
> **(Genesis 1:26)**

God made man in His image. Now, that really tells you something. God didn't make you a lower type of creature. You're not an animal. Your ancestors weren't monkeys. (You may act that way, but that is something you have learned, not how you were created!)

God gave man dominion when He first created him. Look at what God told Adam and Eve in Genesis 1:28:

> **Be fruitful, and multiply, and replenish the earth, and subdue it: and have dominion over the fish of the sea, and over the fowl of the air, and over every living thing that moveth upon the earth.**

One of the main jobs God gave Adam and Eve was to subdue and rule the earth according to His ways and wisdom. This good man and woman had dominion over everything on the entire earth. If they had just obeyed what God said to them, they would still be enjoying their garden paradise.

God also gave the couple **"every herb bearing seed, which is upon the face of all the earth, and every tree, in the which is the fruit of a tree yielding seed"** (Genesis 1:29). You see, originally Adam and Eve didn't have to kill anything or even pray for food; it grew on the trees! Their food didn't have to be prepared, it wasn't cursed, and it came in the right form to eat. The only thing they had to do regarding their food was to plant more seed.

God had provided Adam and Eve with everything they could ever need in the Garden of Eden. Even the temperature was just right. Everything in the Garden, before sin came, was very good. The gold in the Garden was good. In fact, Adam and Eve didn't lack any good thing.

They had abundance. They had peace. They were clothed with the glory and power of God. The light of God was their covering.

Genesis 2:9 gives us even more insight into God's goodness and desire to bless man:

> **Out of the ground made the Lord God to grow every tree that is pleasant to the sight, and good for food; the tree of life also in the midst of the garden, and the tree of knowledge of good and evil.**

God likes things that are "pleasant to the sight"! That's why we have such beautiful countrysides on this earth. That's why in heaven there are flowers and trees and a river and beautiful buildings. God enjoys beauty, and He wants His people to have places in their lives where they can enjoy beauty as well.

Ken and I have lived on the shore of a lake for many years. But even though we have lived there all these years, we still enjoy going down to the boat dock to sit in the swing and watch the sunset together. No matter how many times we have seen the sun set over the lake, we still marvel at its beauty!

It pleases God when you and I enjoy the beauty He has created, especially when we realize that we wouldn't even have any beauty to enjoy if it weren't for the Lord and His goodness. God is good and all good comes from God.

ONE "DO NOT"

In the midst of this abundance, God gave Adam just one "do not." This was the only commandment He gave Adam before sin came, but it was an important one. It was a commandment, not a suggestion.

After placing Adam in the Garden of Eden and instructing him to take care of it, the Lord said to him:

> **Of every tree of the garden thou mayest freely eat:**
> **But of the tree of the knowledge of good and evil, thou**
> **shalt not eat of it: for in the day that thou eatest thereof**
> **thou shalt surely die.**
>
> **(Genesis 2:16-17)**

"Don't eat of this tree of the knowledge of good and evil, for the day you eat of it, you will surely die." That was the only "do not" God asked Adam to obey.

God basically said to Adam, "Here's your beautiful Garden, Adam. Here's your beautiful wife. She's perfect. You're perfect. You are clothed in a beautiful garment of light. Delicious food grows on the trees for you to eat. The temperature is just right.

"I just have this one word for you, Adam: Don't eat of this tree."

That doesn't seem too difficult, does it? That one "do not" was all Adam and Eve had to obey in order to avoid having any problems for the rest of their lives.

But Adam and Eve failed to fulfill that one command. They disobeyed, and in doing so, showed no honor or reverence for God. God had clearly told them what to do, but they chose to allow themselves to be pulled away from God's command, and they ate the forbidden fruit.

THE CHOICE IS OURS

This is the way God operates. He tells you, and you choose. He will not make you do what He wants you to do. God won't make a slave out of anybody. He doesn't want slaves; He wants family.

God also operates by promise. He tells you what will happen if you obey Him and what will happen if you don't obey. And if God says it, you can expect it to happen just that way. God will keep His Word, regardless of the circumstances that surround you.

God kept His Word to Adam and Eve. He didn't intervene, even though He knew exactly what they were doing. He saw them do it. But He didn't come down and say, "No, no, Adam, don't you remember what I told you?"

God let Adam and Eve make their choices. Eve made the first choice to disobey; then Adam made his choice to go with her into sin.

You know, that was a lot for God to give up. That man and woman were all He had other than the angels and His Son.

God made Adam and Eve to have dominion and to replenish the earth. He created the perfect garden for them. He gave them everything they could ever want or need. Then He let them lay it

all on the line, placing all the responsibility on them to obey that one "do not": "Don't eat from that one tree. If you eat, you will surely die."

And notice, God didn't try to explain to Adam all the repercussions of disobeying Him. He didn't relate all the terrible evils that would follow such a tragic decision. He just said, "Don't eat off that one tree."

Why didn't God go into more detail? Well, Adam would probably not have understood too much about how bad dying really is. I mean, Adam had only known life. He had only known good. He had never seen death.

But whether or not Adam understood all the repercussions of disobeying God, he did understand the need to hearken unto Him. If Adam had just hearkened, he would never have eaten of the tree of the knowledge of good and evil.

That was exactly what God wanted for Adam and Eve. He didn't want them to know about evil at all. Now, perhaps in time He would have taught them in His own way. I don't know what He had in mind. Adam and Eve didn't obey Him long enough to find out.

But God wanted to be everything to them. If they had obeyed that one "do not," they would never have known calamity. There would not have been any curse. The devil would never have gained any ground. Adam and Eve and all their descendants would have only known blessing. That was God's will. That's why He told them, "Don't do it!"

But Adam and Eve flunked the test. They disobeyed God. Now, we may think, *Well, I wouldn't have done that if I had lived back then in the Garden of Eden!* But every time we knowingly disobey one of God's commands in His Word, we are doing the same thing Adam and Eve did. Only in hearing what God says and then doing it is there freedom in life. Only then will the devil have no place.

So what happened when the first man and woman disobeyed and ate of the tree of the knowledge of good and evil? They surely died. They didn't die physically; they died spiritually. They were separated from God. Before they had faith and could come freely into God's presence. Now they were afraid and wanted to shrink back from Him. Just as Romans 3:23 says, sin brought them short of God's glory.

HOW THE DEVIL DECEIVES

Let's take a look now at how the devil was able to find an inroad into the lives of Adam and Eve.

> **Now the serpent was more subtle than any beast of the field which the Lord God had made. And he said unto the woman, Yea, hath God said, Ye shall not eat of every tree of the garden?**
>
> **(Genesis 3:1)**

Before the serpent came along, Eve was getting along just fine. She had never even thought about questioning God, and neither had Adam. They both had to have some help to conceive of the possibility that God wasn't telling the truth. They didn't even know what a lie was because no one had ever lied to them!

Adam and Eve knew only one thing: They were not to eat of the tree of the knowledge of good and evil. Then here came the tempter, the devil, speaking to Eve through the serpent. Slyly the serpent planted doubt in Eve's innocent mind with the question,

"Can it really be that God has said, You shall not eat from every tree of the garden?" (Genesis 3:1, AMP).

That's what the devil likes to do (cause people to question God's Word). Satan tries to plant in your mind thoughts of doubt that question the truth of God's promises. For instance, he'll whisper to your mind, *Can it really be that God will heal you? I mean, you've been sick for a long time. Do you really think it's possible that God is going to heal you after you have prayed for so long with no change?*

(Let me answer that one while we're talking about it: Yes, I do believe God will heal you! He loves to perform miracles on long-standing cases. Remember, for example, the old woman in Luke 13:11 who was bowed over for 18 years and could in no wise lift herself up. Jesus healed her, and Jesus wants to heal you! He wants you out of that condition of infirmity, whether you've been that way one day or most of your life.)

Or the devil will whisper to your mind, *Do you really believe God wants to prosper you? Do you really think He wants you to have a nice home or drive a good car? Could it be? Or is it all just Bible talk?*

That's the way the devil operates. He comes to tempt you and talk you out of believing for God's blessings. Your part is to stay determined not to let the devil win.

The devil had to deceive Eve in order to cause her to disobey. His goal was to pull both Adam and Eve into darkness and disobedience, so he could gain a foothold into their lives and subsequently rule the earth. And from the Garden of Eden until the present, nothing has changed in his strategies.

GOD'S WORD OR THE DEVIL'S LIES?

Now let's see how the serpent's conversation with Eve progressed from that first sly question:

> **And the woman said unto the serpent, We may eat
> of the fruit of the trees of the garden: But of the fruit
> of the tree which is in the midst of the garden, God
> hath said, Ye shall not eat of it, neither shall ye touch
> it, lest ye die. And the serpent said unto the woman, Ye
> shall not surely die: For God doth know that in the day
> ye eat thereof, then your eyes shall be opened, and ye
> shall be as gods, knowing good and evil.**
>
> **(Genesis 3:2-5)**

You see, the devil came in gradually. He didn't immediately refer to the forbidden tree of the knowledge of good and evil. He just asked Eve, "Can it be that you shall not eat of every tree in the Garden?" He knew what God had said and repeated it.

But now the devil gets bolder. Having gained a little foothold in the woman's attention, he uses his advantage to plant some doubt in her mind.

Before this, Eve had never known doubt. She had never heard anything but the truth. Adam didn't even speak anything but the truth. She had a perfect husband. Adam had a perfect wife. Everything was good in their lives before the devil came trying to get his foot in the door to make everything bad.

So after gradually "moving in for the kill," the enemy then plainly defies God's words, saying, **"Ye shall not surely die!"**

That's what the devil will do. He'll pull you off the truth a little at a time. Then he'll get you stuck in a mire of trouble, and he won't even try to get you out! That's because the devil can't even do good to people who work for him faithfully. He doesn't have any good in him, so he can't do anyone good.

So what is Eve going to do now? God said she would die if she ate of that tree, and the serpent said she wouldn't.

That's the place believers come to in their spiritual walks all the time—even those who live under the label of "Word people." Over and over again in life, Christians have to choose between what God says and the devil's lies. But if God says, "This is what will happen if you disobey," then I guarantee you, it will happen just as He said.

It's our choice. We have the Word of God, so we have no excuse. Satan may lie to us, saying, "Well, that can't be. Nobody can live that way!" But if God says we can, we can. If God says we should, we must—if we want to walk in the full blessing and glory of God.

The devil lied to Eve. He always lies. If he told the truth, his evil strategies would be doomed. He tells people that God doesn't love them; he tells them things that are not.

Satan does exactly the opposite of what God does. God gives you the choice to hear His Word and do it so He can manifest Himself in your life for your good. On the other hand, the devil tries to trick you into hearing his word and doing it so he can grab control of your life.

GOD'S PLAN: LIFE FREE FROM CALAMITY

After the devil said to Eve, "You shall not surely die," he went on to explain why he claimed that God didn't tell the truth:

For God doth know that in the day ye eat thereof, then your eyes shall be opened, and ye shall be as gods, knowing good and evil.

(Genesis 3:5)

In other words, the devil was enticing Eve with the prospect of choosing her own destiny once she gained the knowledge of good and evil. But that isn't what God originally intended. God wanted His man and woman not to know of calamity or evil. He wants the same for us today. He desires that we live free of the curse of poverty, sickness, sin and disease.

That's why God sent Jesus and put the curse of sin on Him. He took our place and paid our debt so that we can go free from the curse of sin and live a life of blessing and good, free of sin and its evil consequences.

However, the only way to live that kind of life is by doing what God says and operating according to His system rather than the world's system. That means you have to spend a lot of time learning how God thinks and what He says. Every time you learn something new about pleasing and obeying God and incorporate it into your life, you leave the devil less of a foothold and you walk in more and more victory.

That's why I keep on keeping on. That's why I don't quit reading my Bible. I want to know more. I want God to correct me and to show me where I'm missing it. I want to walk in all the blessings He has for me! And I want to be a blessing to Him.

God wanted Adam and Eve to live without even knowing or experiencing calamity. He wanted to be everything to them. He gave them everything they could need or want. He gave them seed so they could continue to maintain their abundant lifestyle. But they let the devil talk them out of it all. As a result, they lost their innocence forever.

INNOCENCE LOST

How did it happen? Let's look at Genesis 3:6 to find out:

> And when the woman saw that the tree was good
> for food, and that it was pleasant to the eyes, and a
> tree to be desired to make one wise, she took of the
> fruit thereof, and did eat, and gave also unto her
> husband with her; and he did eat.

One of the reasons Eve decided to eat the forbidden fruit is because it seemed **"to be desired to make one wise."** The irony of such reasoning is that, if Eve had obeyed God, He would have made her truly wise according to His ways. She could have attained divine wisdom without losing her sinless innocence in the process.

Also, notice that Adam wasn't out playing golf while the serpent was busy tempting Eve. Adam was right there during the entire incident!

> And the eyes of them both were opened, and they
> knew that they were naked; and they sewed fig leaves
> together, and made themselves aprons.
>
> (Genesis 3:7)

Why did Adam and Eve suddenly know that they were naked? Because God's glory had departed from them.

When the Lord came looking for them, Adam told Him, **"I heard thy voice in the garden, and I was afraid, because I was naked; and I hid myself"** (Genesis 3:10).

In other words, Adam knew he was vulnerable. His coat of glory—his garment of light that had clothed him just as God is clothed in light—was suddenly gone. **"Sin entered into the world, and death by sin"** (Romans 5:12). Now he was dead on the inside. Darkness had taken over in his spirit where once there had been light. Death had entered his spirit where once there had been life.

Adam had lost his righteousness before God. He was no longer living in God's ways. He was no longer made as God had made him. He was spiritually dead.

Sin brought Adam and Eve short of the glory of God. The day they ate, they surely died. No, they didn't die physically for many hundreds of years. But they died spiritually at that moment. They became separated from God.

"GET OUT OF MY GARDEN!"

When the Lord asked Adam why he had eaten the forbidden fruit, Adam had an answer: **"The woman whom thou gavest to be with me, she gave me of the tree, and I did eat"** (Genesis 3:12).

It was the woman's fault.

Then the Lord asked Eve why she had disobeyed. Eve also had an answer: **"The serpent beguiled me, and I did eat"** (v. 13).

It was the serpent's fault.

Blame it on somebody else. That's what people want to do when they get in trouble. That's what Adam and Eve did.

But Adam had no one to blame but himself. He could have redeemed the situation. He could have rebuked that serpent when the creature began to question the Word of God. Adam could have told the serpent, "Get out of my garden!"

That was Adam's place. You see, God had given him dominion over every creeping thing. He had commanded Adam to rule and subdue the earth. But Adam didn't do it. He didn't take any action to get rid of the danger. Instead, he chose to go the wrong way.

Adam had authority over the devil. The Garden of Eden belonged to Adam and Eve; God had given it to them. Therefore, it was not only Adam's right but his duty to rebuke and banish the serpent that was contradicting God's Word.

There's an important lesson to be learned here. When the devil tries to beguile you, refuse to allow yourself to think or meditate on his lies. Don't even begin to think, *What if?* or *Will God?* Don't get off the Word of God at all.

Doubt or temptation will try to pull you off God's path into sin every time. But you are to cast down every high imagination that exalts itself against the knowledge of God (2 Corinthians 10:5). Don't think about it, toy with it or tolerate it. Instead, rebuke it and cast it out!

That is your right and your responsibility. You don't even have to think about it. The moment thoughts of doubt begin to erode God's Word in your life, command them to get out in the Name of Jesus. Say, "Get out, you little doubt devil! Get out of my presence! I won't tolerate unbelief. I refuse to be disrespectful to my Father. I will tolerate no word that contradicts the Word of God in my life!"

Don't let the devil take control of your life by yielding to his strategies and disobeying God's Word. Don't let depression come on you. Don't let your past rise up to overcome you. You've been redeemed from your past if you are born again. The blood of Jesus covers your past, cleanses you from all unrighteousness, remits your sin and sets you free! Now you don't have to make the mistake Adam did.

THE CONSEQUENCES OF DISOBEDIENCE

Adam didn't exercise his rightful authority. Instead, he hearkened to his wife and disobeyed God, eating from the tree of which

God had said, **"Thou shalt not eat."** That decision would cost him dearly.

God pronounced the consequences that would result from Adam's disobedience:

> **Cursed is the ground for thy sake; in sorrow shalt thou eat of it all the days of thy life; Thorns also and thistles shall it bring forth to thee; and thou shalt eat the herb of the field; In the sweat of thy face shalt thou eat bread, till thou return unto the ground; for out of it wast thou taken: for dust thou art, and unto dust shalt thou return.**
>
> **(Genesis 3:17-19)**

From this moment on, the curse of sin came upon earth's soil. It would no longer produce food that satisfied man without labor and struggle. Thorns and thistles would begin to grow, ever threatening to choke the crops man tried to plant and cultivate.

Adam and Eve were also put out of the Garden lest they eat of the tree of life and stay in that sinful condition forever. The first couple left that perfect environment to eke out an existence under the curse, living the way natural man has to live—digging his livelihood out of this earth by the sweat of his brow.

Sin had changed everything—not only the man and woman, but the world in which they lived.

RESTORED TO OUR ORIGINAL POSITION

But God changed all that when He sent Jesus to redeem us. When we are born again, we stop being just natural men and women. We become born of God. We are restored to a position

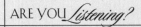

of dominion—over sickness, death, weakness, pain, poverty and every strategy of the enemy.

Jesus has restored man to his original position with God. Man once again can come before God after he makes Jesus Christ the Lord of his life. He can come up to the very throne room of God and find grace to help in time of trouble (Hebrews 4:16).

We can approach God. We can hear from God. We can be led by God. We can be filled with God. We can have the garment of God's glory covering us once more—*if* we will but hear and do what God says.

You know, that one "if" includes a lot. Most of all, it means taking the time to find out what God has to say. You have to hear it before you can do it! That's why faith comes by hearing and hearing by the Word of God (Romans 10:17).

Hearing and doing the Word of God has been a crucial part of God's plan for man from the very beginning. And God desires the same thing for us as He desired for the first man and woman. He wants us to come to a place in our spiritual walk where we hear and obey Him, so the devil can find no foothold in our lives. Therefore, calamity can't touch us and nothing can stand between us and victory!

SATAN'S WORST NIGHTMARE: THE GLORIOUS CHURCH

Satan knows his time as god of this world system is almost over. But he still tries to keep everyone out of the power and glory and blessing of God. He knows there is something about a victorious person that causes multiplication.

You see, people want victory. When they see victory in our lives, they want it in their lives. That's why the devil tries to keep us all poor-mouthed and defeated. Then no one will want to be like us.

But that day is gone forever! The light of God's Word is shining brighter and brighter. More and more people are hearing the Word with the intent to do it. More and more are being blessed, healed and made prosperous. Others are seeing it and saying, "I want whatever you have!"

The devil desperately fights that kind of situation. If there has to be a Church, he certainly doesn't want it to be a glorious Church! That's his worst nightmare!

But that's exactly what the devil will have to face. I'm telling you, we're not going out of here limping and defeated! We're going out of here in victory and power. We're going out of here only after we have taken dominion over the devil's works in the earth! We are going out the victorious Church.

Above all, God wants you to be free. That freedom is found only in the Word of God. The more you hear, the more you do. And the more you do, the freer you become to experience God's best!

Prayer of Consecration

Lord, You wanted to do good to Adam and Eve all the days of their lives. You wanted to be God to them, to provide for them, to teach them, to empower them. And You want the same for me. So I offer myself up to You, Lord. I want You to have the place of dominion in my life. I choose You to be God in every area of my life. I choose Your Son, Jesus, to be my Savior and the Lord of my life.

THINK ON THESE THINGS

God won't make a slave out of anybody.
He doesn't want slaves; He wants family.

Only in hearing what God says and then doing it is there freedom in
life. Only then will the devil have no place.

When we are born again, we stop being just natural men and women.
We become born of God. We are restored to
a position of dominion—over sickness, death, weakness,
pain, poverty and every strategy of the enemy.

We can have the garment of God's glory covering us
once more—if we will but hear and do what God says.

CHAPTER 4

GOD'S MESSAGE
TO ISRAEL:
"HEARKEN"

God treated Israel the very same way He did Adam and Eve. He told Moses exactly what Israel was to do. He promised the Israelites nothing short of total victory if they would obey Him. God said, "If you will do what I say, you will possess everything I have ever promised you!"

IT'S EASIER FOR US TO OBEY GOD

Now we actually have a lot more to do for God's kingdom than Israel had to do. For one thing, in these last days it's our responsibility to take the gospel to the ends of the earth before Jesus returns (Matthew 24:14).

But we have a distinct advantage, too. As believers, we have hearts of flesh, not of stone. Speaking of the new covenant that was to come, God promised, **"I will give them one heart, and I will put a new spirit within you; and I will take the stony heart out of their flesh, and will give them an heart of flesh"** (Ezekiel 11:19).

We have the capacity to walk in a dimension of power and victory that Israel didn't have. It's easier for us to do what we are

called to do than it was for them, because they had unregenerate, sinful hearts, and we are new creations in Christ Jesus.

In fact, we have less of an excuse than anyone under the old covenant for not hearing and doing what God has told us to do. God sent us His Spirit to live in us, to strengthen us, to help us and to teach us. What was His purpose in doing that? So we could walk out everything He has called us to do.

You have the Teacher living inside you. If you want to get out of bed and receive revelation from the Word of God in the middle of the night, you can. You can pull out your Bible and say, "Here I am, Holy Spirit. Show me what You have for me in this Word." Then you can just start fellowshiping with God in the spirit.

What a privilege it is to have that kind of access to God! We really have no excuses. God has given us every tool and every avenue to be strong in Him and to obey His Word.

HEAR AND DO DILIGENTLY

Let's take a journey through the book of Deuteronomy. I want to show you how God's message to hearken is interwoven throughout everything that happened to Israel.

Deuteronomy 4:1 sets the tone of God's recurring message to Israel:

> **Now therefore hearken, O Israel, unto the statutes and unto the judgments, which I teach you, for to do them, that ye may live, and go in and possess the land which the Lord God of your fathers giveth you.**

What was Israel's part to fulfill in order to go in and possess the land? They had to take the basic Bible course to victory; they had to *hear and do.*

The children of Israel were learning the same lesson that we have to learn today: Every time they held back from obeying God, they gave defeat a place in their lives. On the other hand, every time they stepped forward by faith and did what God told them to, they gave victory a place to manifest. It was—and is— just that simple.

> **Keep therefore and do them** [God's statutes]**; for this is your wisdom and your understanding in the sight of the nations, which shall hear all these statutes, and say, Surely this great nation is a wise and understanding people.**
>
> **(Deuteronomy 4:6)**

Keep God's words and do them. That was to be the key to Israel's demonstration of divine wisdom and understanding in the sight of all nations.

God told His people exactly how to live, what to do, what to eat, how to conduct themselves, how to worship and how to give. He wanted them to stand out as something special because He wanted every nation to know that there was a God in Israel. He wanted His people to be a witness to Him.

If you are a parent, you should understand God's desire. Don't you want your child to stand out as someone special? You don't want your child to be backward, weak and defeated. No, you want your child to shine! You want him to be a winner.

Well, God feels the same way. He wants His children to have the best, be the best, love the best, obey the best and hear the best.

So in this scripture, He tells Israel how to shine. Keeping and doing the Word would be their demonstration of wisdom—the one thing that would cause other nations to say, "This is a wise people."

But it couldn't be a haphazard effort. In Deuteronomy 4:9, 29, God tells the children of Israel what it would take for them to walk in wisdom and to make their way prosperous:

> **Only take heed to thyself, and *keep thy soul diligently*, lest thou forget the things which thine eyes have seen, and lest they depart from thy heart all the days of thy life: but teach them thy sons, and thy sons' sons....**
>
> **But if from thence thou shalt seek the Lord thy God, thou shalt find him, *if thou seek him with all thy heart and with all thy soul*.**

In order to make God's Word work for themselves, the Israelites would have to be diligent about letting God be God in their lives. They would have to seek Him with all their hearts and souls.

The same is true today. We have to be diligent in order to live a bold lifestyle of faith, because the world around us is going in a different direction. For each of us, obeying God's Word has to become our whole life. God has to be the first thing we think about in the morning and the last thing we think about at night. His ways have to find place in our hearts until everything we do—even the little things—are overshadowed by the Word of God.

THE FATHER'S COMMAND TO OBEY IS FOR OUR GOOD

The Father has always wanted a family who would let Him be their Father. He says to His children, "Hey, I'm for you. I'm not against you. I want to help you. I want to be everything to you."

God wants to be a Father to you. He wants to meet your every need. But to let Him be your Father, you have to hear His Word and then obey it. Then He can take His place as Father,

Provider and *El Shaddai* to you. He can exhibit all of His wonderful, loving, caring and compassionate attributes in your life.

God desired to do just that in the Garden. He wanted to provide for Adam and Eve. He wanted to make their lives good and to provide them with every possible blessing. But there was one thing that they had to do. To abide in that place of good and blessing and increase, they had to *do what He said*.

So here He is again, in Deuteronomy—another time with another generation, but God is still endeavoring to teach His people the same thing: To experience victory and blessing, you have to *hear and do*.

You see, the reason God commands His people to obey is not because He is a tyrant who always wants his own way. God is a good God, and He wants His children to be free. So He gave Israel certain commands to obey, saying:

> **Thou shalt keep therefore his statutes, and his commandments, which I command thee this day, that it may go well with thee, and with thy children after thee, and that thou mayest prolong thy days upon the earth, which the Lord thy God giveth thee, for ever.**
>
> **(Deuteronomy 4:40)**

That's the reason God gives us His Word. He wants everything to go well with us generation after generation and so that we may prolong our days.

God knows what works. He doesn't want us to die young and fail to finish the spiritual race He has set before us. Many scriptures tell us that He wants us to live a long, good life on the earth (Psalm 91:16; Ephesians 6:2-3). So God tells us in no uncertain terms, **"Ye shall observe to do therefore as the Lord**

your God hath commanded you: ye shall not turn aside to the right hand or to the left" (Deuteronomy 5:32).

Let's skip ahead to Deuteronomy 8:1 for a moment because it pertains to this point. God tells His people, **"All the commandments which I command thee this day shall ye observe to do, that ye may live."**

That was always God's desire and intention. He wanted the children of Israel to enjoy a good life in which He could be everything they needed. So He gave them His Word and told them exactly what to do.

God says something similar in Deuteronomy 6:18:

> **And thou shalt do that which is right and good in the sight of the Lord: that it may be well with thee, and that thou mayest go in and possess the good land which the Lord sware unto thy fathers.**

In the natural, this is not a well earth. But when God moves in to shine His light in our lives, things begin to go well with us.

God gives us His wisdom—His way of doing and being right— so that it may be well with us. As we walk in that divine wisdom, God is free to operate in our lives to make it well with us.

That's how you honor God. You pay attention to what He says, and then you obey Him. You keep His ways, operating in what He says is right, so that you may live a good life and prolong your days.

THE WORD IS A TWO-EDGED SWORD

God wants to bless His people, but it all depends on whether or not they heed His message to hear and do. In Deuteronomy

4:26, God warns Israel about what will happen if they don't take heed: **"Ye shall soon utterly perish from off the land whereunto ye go over Jordan to possess it; ye shall not prolong your days upon it, but shall utterly be destroyed."**

Remember, the Word is called a *two*-edged sword (Hebrews 4:12). It cuts both ways. It cuts in your favor if you obey it, but it cuts to your sorrow if you don't obey it. Is that fair? Absolutely! God tells us what to do to be blessed, and He tells us what will cause us to miss out on His blessings.

It's a question of whether or not you give Him first place as God in your life. That means He is to be number one in your priorities. He is to be everything to you. What He says becomes a way of life to you. His words are your truth for you to live by.

Deuteronomy 4:29 shows the mercy side of the "two-edged sword": **"But if from thence thou shalt seek the Lord thy God, thou shalt find him, if thou seek him with all thy heart and with all thy soul."**

That's typical of God. You will find throughout the Bible that God always tells His people what to do to reverse the curse. He tells them the terrible things that will happen to them if they rebel against Him. Then He always tries to call them back from their disobedient ways, to convince them to let go of their iniquities so He can save them.

A HEART TO HEAR AND DO

Many times God's people were disloyal. They often even worshiped other gods. But when they repented and turned back to Him, God was always there for them, with compassion and grace, waiting to take them back.

It's amazing how many times Israel turned against God when He had done so much for them. Think about it. God delivered the children of Israel out of slavery through miraculous signs and wonders. While terrible plagues came on Egypt because they defied God, He loaded His people down with silver and gold, healed all who were sick and brought them out without even one feeble one among their tribes (Psalm 105:37). He parted the Red Sea and supernaturally gave them the Ten Commandments.

After all that, you'd think Israel would at least do what God said, wouldn't you? But they still wouldn't obey. God looked at them and said, **"O that there were such an heart in them, that they would fear me, and keep all my commandments always, that it might be well with them, and with their children for ever!"** (Deuteronomy 5:29).

That scripture reveals God's heart. He knows that the fear and reverence of the Lord is the beginning of wisdom. If a person doesn't have the fear of God, he won't ever walk in God's wisdom. He will always think he knows better, or that the world knows better—or that *somebody* knows better than God does.

When you walk in the fear and reverence of God, you have a heart to hear and do. You honor Him, whether that's what you want for your life or not, whether you agree with what He says or not. When God says it, you do it—simply because you reverence Him. When you honor God like that, He promises that it will be well with you and your children forever!

THE GIFT OF A LEADER

The children of Israel didn't obey very well on their own. They were in great need of a leader. So God called Moses as a teacher and told him to teach Israel His ways. It says in Deuteronomy 5:1:

> **Moses called all Israel, and said unto them, Hear, O Israel, the statutes and judgments which I speak in your ears this day, that ye may learn them, and keep, and do them.**

Learn, keep and do God's Word. The teacher has just given his pupils the key they need for success.

In Deuteronomy 5:31, God confirmed Moses' role as a leader and a teacher:

> **But as for thee, stand thou here by me, and I will speak unto thee all the commandments, and the statutes, and the judgments, which thou shalt teach them, that they may do them in the land which I give them to possess it.**

Moses was supposed to teach the people what God had told him. If the people did as they were taught, they would inherit the Promised Land.

YOU DON'T HAVE TO UNDERSTAND TO OBEY

That didn't mean the Israelites always understood what God told them to do. They didn't. But God expected them to obey His commandments and trust Him to be God in their lives.

We don't always understand what God tells us to do either. We may wonder, *How will it all come together? Where's the money coming from? How long will it be?* But God usually doesn't answer all those questions for us right away. He hardly ever lays out all the details from the outset of something He tells us to do. He wants us to walk by faith and not by sight. We have to trust Him.

You just have to get used to the way God operates. You do that by spending so much time in the Word that you don't fear for your future anymore. You're not afraid to step out of the boat and commit to something, because you're confident that God will help you see it through to the end.

You only get to that strong place of faith by fellowshiping with God in the Word and in prayer. The only way you *stay* strong in faith is by continually spending time in the Word for the rest of your life!

Stay teachable. Proverbs 4:20 says, **"My son, attend to my words; incline thine ear unto my saying."** Keep going to meetings where the Word is preached. Keep listening to people of strong faith who stay connected to their Heavenly Father. Let the Word of God convince you that God is faithful, whether you understand His way of doing things or not!

KNOWING AND WALKING IN GOD'S WAYS

In Deuteronomy 5:33, we find Moses once again pointing the way to victory for the Israelites:

> **Ye shall walk in all the ways which the Lord your God hath commanded you, that ye may live, and that it may be well with you, and that ye may prolong your days in the land which ye shall possess.**

What was the prerequisite for long life and for things going well in the land Israel would possess? They had to *walk in God's ways.*

You know, it's a wonderful thing that God has given us revelation of His ways—how He thinks and what He says is right. We won't find victory any other place, except in the knowledge of His ways.

But it's not just knowledge that is important; it's *acting* on that knowledge. Some people sit through Bible school from two to four years. Then after graduation, they go out and fail to act on a single thing they learned in school! And only to the extent they do the things they have learned from God will they have victory.

A TREASURE HUNT FOR TRUTH

Ken and I learned that principle early in our faith walk, more than 32 years ago. We were desperate. We wanted help. We wanted out of trouble. We had been in financial bondage way too long. So when we found out that the Word of God held our key to victory, we went on a treasure hunt into its pages.

Nothing else was important to us. We didn't know what was on television or at the movie theater. We didn't know what was happening in the news. We didn't focus our attention on anything except the life-saving revelation that freedom comes from hearing and doing the Word.

When Kenneth and I first embarked on this spiritual treasure hunt, we agreed together and said, "OK, whatever we see in the Word, we're going to do it!" That's exactly what we have endeavored to do ever since. We haven't fulfilled that goal perfectly, but we have been diligent in our pursuit of God's ways. When we do fail, we repent and go again—always going toward more of God. As a result, we have walked in victory.

We want to be more victorious this year than we were last year! We want to know more of the Word of God. We want to be more obedient than we have ever been, with the desire always to be more like Him!

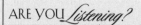

EXPECT TO INCREASE *MIGHTILY!*

Let's look at another good reason which Moses gave Israel to hear and do God's Word.

> **Hear therefore, O Israel, and observe to do it; that it may be well with thee, and that ye may *increase mightily*, as the Lord God of thy fathers hath promised thee, in the land that floweth with milk and honey.**
>
> **(Deuteronomy 6:3)**

Again and again, throughout the Bible, we see that God is always wanting His people to increase.

God had promised increase to His covenant people. His heart's desire was to be able to fulfill that promise of increase given to Abraham. He promised Abraham and his seed the land and the blessing of increase.

Consider Abraham's life for a moment. God promised Abraham that he would be rich, and that promise came to pass. Genesis 13:2 says, **"Abram was very rich in cattle, in silver, and in gold."** No one could rule or reign over Abraham. He was the head and not the tail.

Abraham increased *mightily* in the land where the Lord brought him. That was God's desire. And that's what God wants to do for the seed of Abraham even today.

The Scripture says in Galatians 3:29 that as heirs of Christ, *we* are the seed of Abraham. All those covenant promises which God made to Abraham and to the generations after him are still alive. God endeavored through the years to get His people in a position to receive from Him. He now desires the same for us.

God wants to fulfill His promises in our lives. But we have to decide that we'll be in that group of believers who obey God and enjoy the fulfillment of God's promise to Abraham—increase in every area of life!

TEACH YOUR CHILDREN DILIGENTLY

One of the most important aspects of hearkening to God's Word is making sure His truth is passed on to the next generation. Moses stressed this principle to the children of Israel in Deuteronomy 6:6-7:

> **And these words, which I command thee this day, shall be in thine heart:** *And thou shalt teach them diligently unto thy children,* **and shalt talk of them when thou sittest in thine house, and when thou walkest by the way, and when thou liest down, and when thou risest up.**

Raise your children on the Word of God. Teach them that they can believe God for anything! Make sure this message of faith is passed on in your family, from generation to generation.

Notice in this scripture *when* you are supposed to speak the Word to your children: when you sit, when you walk, when you lie down and when you rise up. Any other time, you can say what you want!

Now, I think some people believe that verse is talking about when to watch television, because that's just about how much they watch it every day! But the Bible doesn't say, "Let television teach your children"; it says that you are to teach your children the Word. Throughout the day, talk to your family and to one another about God and the great things He is doing!

Do you know what causes your children to get the most out of what you teach them? Seeing a manifestation of those truths with their own eyes! They will never forget a miracle once they have seen one for themselves.

When our son, John, was just about 3 years old, Ken and I were believing for a station wagon. We had been standing in faith for that station wagon for months and months.

Kenneth would say all the time, "Thank God for our new car." One day John asked, "Daddy, do we have a new car?"

"Yes, Son, we do. We believe we receive a new car."

Puzzled, John asked, "Well, then, why don't we go get it?"

Kenneth couldn't show that station wagon to John right then and there. But the day did come when John saw our family enjoy that new station wagon!

Our children remember how their parents received by faith what our family needed as they grew up. They have never known anything but faith in the Word of God. Today they operate the same way with their children. And because our kids started as parents at a higher spiritual level than Ken and I did, their children are growing even faster spiritually than they did.

Now, that doesn't mean our children never went through any struggles as they grew up. But Ken and I found out that if we would live what we preached before them, our godly example would influence them long after they left home to live on their own.

For example, when John was a teenager, he really didn't aspire to be a preacher's child. He was all boy and wanted to do all those "boy things." He didn't think he wanted to follow in his father's footsteps. But he couldn't get away from all he had learned, and he couldn't deny the fact that his parents had lived what they had preached at home.

John had seen prayer work all his life. He had seen how we believed God for our needs to be met, refusing to get in fear when bad circumstances hit. John had witnessed for himself that when we made mistakes, we repented and made things right. He didn't have any question about whether or not there was anything to this faith walk we preached about.

After he graduated from high school, John moved out on his own and started doing some things he shouldn't have. But even though he wasn't living for God at the time, John always had a good heart.

One night John called his daddy and said, "Dad, I want to talk to you." He came over to our house, and talking to Kenneth, he said, "You know, Dad, things haven't been going right for me and I want to give you my tithe."

Where did John's conviction to tithe come from? We had instilled that in him, not as much by what we *said* as by what we *did*. John grew up watching our example of tithing, no matter what.

That's what the Bible means when it says, **"Train up a child in the way he should go: and when he is old, he will not depart from it"** (Proverbs 22:6). Which way should your child go? God's way. And if you live a right example before that child all of his days, he won't be able to stray from that godly training for very long.

Of course, all our children, including John, are committed today, on fire for God and working in the ministry. And our grandchildren are disciples taught of the Lord. God is faithful!

What would have happened if Kenneth and I hadn't practiced what we preached at home? I don't believe we would have the same good testimony about our children.

You see, your kids hear everything you preach. And I guarantee you, they will judge you by it if you are one way at home and another way at church.

So help your children grow up respecting the things of God. When you make a mistake, let your children hear you repent. Tell them, "I was wrong. I want you to know I repent, and I ask you to forgive me." Don't be afraid to get real before your children.

I have seen the good results in families where parents live as godly examples before their kids. Parents like that are raising up a generation of children who know God and know how to get answers to their prayers.

The "Superkid Academy" is the children's church at Eagle Mountain International Church in Fort Worth. The children there aren't just hearing Bible stories. They are prophesying and laying hands on the sick. They are hearing the voice of God. They are experiencing Holy Ghost services. They are seeing miracles!

It is awesome to behold what God is doing among the children of this day. That comes from diligently teaching them the Word and living that Word before them!

GOD'S WILL IS ABUNDANCE!

Deuteronomy 6:10-12 gives us a better picture of what God desired to give the children of Israel:

> **And it shall be, when the Lord thy God shall have brought thee into the land which he sware unto thy fathers, to Abraham, to Isaac, and to Jacob, to give thee great and goodly cities, which thou buildest not, And houses full of all good things, which thou filledst not, and wells digged, which thou diggedst not, vineyards**

and olive trees, which thou plantedst not; when thou shalt have eaten and be full; Then beware lest thou forget the Lord, which brought thee forth out of the land of Egypt, from the house of bondage.

God always wanted His people to have an abundance of everything. He wanted them to have wealth and prosperity and healing and peace and joy. But there was just one prerequisite: He had to be God to them.

God was telling Israel, "Let Me be God in your life. That's the only way you will receive all the good things I have for you. It's the only way you will enjoy peace, stand before your enemies and prolong your days. Just do what I say, and your victory is guaranteed."

I'm telling you, that's a revelation that will take you on home! *Your victory is guaranteed when you do what God says.*

On the other hand, we probably all know people who continually seem to be encountering some kind of traumatic test. They may be lovely, sweet people who attend Word conventions all the time and can quote the Bible. But they live their daily lives as if the Word isn't true for *them.* They don't take hold of what belongs to them, so instead of enjoying victory, they are always facing trouble. They are hearers and not doers of the Word.

God wanted victory and abundance for His people Israel, and He still wants the same for the seed of Abraham today. *Nothing* is too hard for God when He has someone who will just let Him work in his or her life.

You know, sometimes it taxes our faith just to believe for a house. But in this scripture, God isn't just talking about giving *houses* to His people. God doesn't deal only in houses or even in city blocks. God thinks in terms of *cities* and *nations.*

So do you think a God Who is willing to give His people cities, and even nations, would stagger at paying your bills or solving your problems? You simply can't overtax God with what you need or desire.

GOD'S VIEW ON REAL ESTATE

Now, notice what God says about the cities He was giving His people. These cities had houses full of all good things just waiting for the Israelites to live in once they possessed the land (v. 11)! After reading this scripture, would you think that it was God's will for you to own land and live in a house full of good things? Absolutely!

Think about it. We're under a better covenant than the Israelites were, and God offered them cities and vineyards and wells and houses full of good things. I believe with all my heart that God wants nothing less for us.

Real estate is very important to God. He wants His children to own land and have homes in which to live. After all, God made this earth for His family. In fact, I'll even say this: Anyone who has a piece of this earth that God didn't give him is actually living on land that doesn't belong to him!

How can I say that? Because even though the devil thinks the earth is his, it isn't. The Bible says the whole earth and everything in it belong to God (Psalm 24:1). Well, only the owner has the right to give the deed to his property to someone else. If I were to give you a house that wasn't mine to give, you wouldn't be living there very long!

Therefore, every piece of real estate on this planet still belongs to God unless He has already given that specific title deed to someone.

If you study the account of the Israelites' travels through the wilderness to the Promised Land, you will find that God does give land to people. Israel journeyed through places where God said, "Don't bother these people. Pay for anything you receive from them. I will not give you this land because I have already given it to so-and-so (a specific person)."

But of the Promised Land, He said, "You will dispossess these people, for I have given the land and all that is in it to you" (See Deuteronomy 2:4-9 and Numbers 33:52-53, author's paraphrase). In this case, the people lost the land they lived in because of sin and disobedience. They had no covenant with God. He hadn't given them the title deed to that property.

The earth belongs to God, and He wants His family to have it. This wasn't a new revelation for Israel. God told Adam to subdue and have dominion over the earth. It has always been His will to give His people real estate. God wanted to give His people the Promised Land, so He told them to go in and possess it. All the people had to do was hear His words and obey them.

So if you are believing God for property or for a new home, this is the time to hear and do! There is great revelation going forth in this day. Never has there been an hour in the history of the Church when believing God for property was easier than it is right now.

If you see a piece of property and God quickens to your spirit that He wants you to have it, jump out there and believe Him for it! God can bring it into your hands if you will walk by faith. You don't have to work it all out; all you have to do is know when to act on what you hear. (Of course, be sure not to covet what belongs to someone else. If it is not for sale, leave it in the Lord's hands. He has something just for you!)

EAGLE MOUNTAIN: SET ASIDE FOR DIVINE PURPOSES

I can testify from my own experience that just as God prepared a fruitful land for the children of Israel to possess, He prepares land and homes for His children today.

For instance, God prepared and set aside the land out at Eagle Mountain for our ministry. It's a wonderful piece of property that encompasses 1,522 acres. The government owned it for a long time. Then an elderly gentleman bought it and kept it undeveloped for many years. Finally, when the owner was more than 80 years old, Kenneth went out to talk to him and let him know that the Lord needed that land. (That's what the Lord told him to say.)

You see, one day 11 years earlier, Ken happened to be flying over that land, and God spoke to him about it. The Lord told Ken that He had plans for that piece of property.

So the land sat and waited for 11 years. Then one day God told Kenneth it was time to go talk to the owner. Kenneth didn't have the money to buy the land at the time. But God had told him what to do, so Kenneth obeyed. And eventually the owner came up with a plan. It was God's plan!

The owner told Kenneth, "You pay $25,000 a month for the land as a lease. Then buy the land whenever you want to, one quarter section at a time. When you're ready to purchase the last section of property, I'll apply every penny you've paid in lease payments to the balance due."

God had prepared that land for us and kept it until the right time came. God has prepared a place for you! Just make sure your faith is strong and ready to act when the opportunity comes and God tells you what to do to possess it.

Proverbs 13:22 says, **"The wealth of the sinner is laid up for the just."** That scripture is being fulfilled in this hour. Natural possessions are moving out of the kingdom of darkness and into the kingdom of light. God is making supernatural transfers of money, gold, property and goods from the world to the Church.

I'm telling you, this is the hour of property! God wants His people who hear and obey His Word to live in abundance and to fulfill His purposes in these last days. He has something He wants us to do, and we're going to do it! He knows our future. He knows what we will need in order to fulfill what He has called us to do. And that includes possessing the home or property He has prepared for us!

RIGHTEOUSNESS AND OBEDIENCE

Now let's move on to Deuteronomy 6:25, where Moses makes a profound statement to Israel:

And it shall be our righteousness, if we observe to do all these commandments before the Lord our God, as he hath commanded us.

Under the old covenant, God counted His people righteous when they did what He said.

But we have a much greater advantage than the children of Israel did! On the inside we have been re-created as the righteousness of God (2 Corinthians 5:21). To live a lifestyle of hearing and obeying God should be natural for us!

Look at Matthew 6:33. In the *Amplified* version it says:

But seek (aim at and strive after) first of all His kingdom and His righteousness (His way of doing and

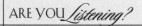

being right), and then all these things taken together will be given you besides.

"Seek Me first." Those three words are a good summation of what God was always saying to the children of Israel. The Israelites were to seek God's way of doing and being right. And if they did what He told them to, God would count it as righteousness before Him.

You may be born again in righteousness under the new covenant, but you still have to wear the robe of righteousness. In other words, you must live a righteous, obedient life, day by day, in order to open the way for God to bless you.

Some Christians try to live a double life, serving God only when it's convenient. But although they may fool some people, they can't fool the One Who is the answer to all their needs. They also don't fool themselves. Abiding peace is only found in someone who lives uprightly in obedience before God.

So don't hang out with those who live an unrighteous lifestyle. Fellowship with people who hear and obey the Word. It will help you to stay headed in the right direction.

And, remember, hearing the Word is not enough to receive the blessings of God. Just like the Israelites, you must *hearken* to the Word with the intent to *do!*

Prayer of Consecration

Lord, I want to walk with You in the kingdom of God on this earth. I give You my loyalty. I give You my honor. I reverence Your every word.

I thank You for expanding my thinking to expect an increase— both of Your glory and of this earth's goods—manifested in my life. Thank You for causing me to live in a spiritual land where there is no scarcity or lack!

THINK ON THESE THINGS

*God has given us every tool and every avenue
to be strong in Him and to obey His Word.*

*Let the Word of God convince you that God is faithful,
whether you understand His way of doing things or not!*

Your victory is guaranteed when you do what God says.

*Nothing is too hard for God when He has someone
who will just let Him work in his or her life.*

CHAPTER 5

I hope you are starting to get the picture that God has blessings on His mind for you—and not just a little sprinkle of blessings. He has a flood of blessings He wants to pour into your life, if you will just hear Him and obey what He says.

ALL MEANS *ALL*

Let me show you what I mean by a flood of blessings. Look at Deuteronomy 7:13-15:

> **And he will love thee, and bless thee, and multiply thee: he will also bless the fruit of thy womb, and the fruit of thy land, thy corn, and thy wine, and thine oil, the increase of thy kine, and the flocks of thy sheep, in the land which he sware unto thy fathers to give thee.**

> **Thou shalt be blessed above all people: there shall not be male or female barren among you, or among your cattle.**

> **And the Lord will take away from thee all sickness, and will put none of the evil diseases of Egypt, which thou knowest, upon thee; but will lay them upon all them that hate thee.**

Now, I don't know about you, but I conclude from these verses that God wants His people to be blessed, increased, favored, securely situated and prospered—above all people!

I love that word *all*. You just can't argue with it. All means *all!* The way God planned it, there should be nothing left on the other side to even compare with the blessings God's people enjoy!

And notice in verse 15 that God's blessings include being free from all sickness and disease. (There's that word *all* again!) Divine health is a part of the increase that God will multiply unto us as we hearken to obey His Word.

Too many of God's people have hunkered down under the world's system, letting its defeated way of thinking dictate what they can and can't have. Meanwhile, throughout these thousands of years, God has been saying all along what He really wants to do: "I want to bless you above *all* people!"

The world hasn't seen a fraction of the blessings God wants to heap upon His people. As that begins to change, we will see a great increase of souls born into the kingdom of God.

You see, worldly people are rather fickle. Often they don't have an allegiance to anything except their own desires to do better for themselves. That's why when people see God's blessings upon a church, they aren't picky about what is being preached. They don't even care if the church people talk in tongues or fall on the floor when they are prayed for! When people see that they can get healed or delivered at that church, they will go!

That's an altogether different attitude than religious people have. Those who are religious don't want you to do or say anything that disagrees with what they are already doing, or that is out of line with their tradition.

But the world wants relief and help. People just want to experience blessing instead of pain.

And that lines up exactly with God's heart. He desires to manifest Himself in our lives, causing blessings where there were once only curses, healing where there was once only sickness and abundance where there was once only poverty. God wants to be the Light that overwhelms the darkness in every area of our lives until we are blessed above all people!

Deuteronomy 28:13 says it another way:

The Lord shall make thee the head, and not the tail; and thou shalt be above only, and thou shalt not be beneath; if that thou hearken unto the commandments of the Lord thy God, which I command thee this day, to observe and to do them.

When you're the head, people around you know it. You can't hide a continual increase in peace, joy, material goods and finances! On the other hand, people around you also know it when you are the tail, and they are not impressed with that situation. They are already struggling to make it through life; they don't need to learn from you how to do that! But they would like to learn how to receive all the blessings.

Deuteronomy 7:17-19 gives us one more way God wants to bless us above all people. He wants to cause us to stand victorious over every strategy of the enemy!

If thou shalt say in thine heart, These nations are more than I; how can I dispossess them? Thou shalt not be afraid of them: but shalt well remember what the Lord thy God did unto Pharaoh, and unto all Egypt; The great temptations which thine eyes saw, and

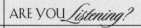
**the signs, and the wonders, and the mighty hand, and
the stretched out arm, whereby the Lord thy God brought
thee out: so shall the Lord thy God do unto all the
people of whom thou art afraid.**

The children of Israel didn't have to be afraid of anyone.
They had God on their side! But remember, the prerequisite God
established for that kind of divine protection was not just that
they were His covenant people. They had to walk in His ways,
letting Him be God and tell them how to live. They had to hear
and do.

GOD PROVES US

God's eyes were on His people as they traveled through the
wilderness. Deuteronomy 8:16 says that this was a time of proving
for Israel. God sought to know what was in their hearts.

**And he humbled thee, and suffered thee to hunger,
and fed thee with manna, which thou knewest not,
neither did thy fathers know; that he might make thee
know that man doth not live by bread only, but by
every word that proceedeth out of the mouth of the
Lord doth man live.**

(Deuteronomy 8:3)

There are times of proving for us as well, looking to see what
is in our hearts when it is not easy to obey. We have to be willing
to walk by faith in what God says instead of by what we see in
the natural. The Bible says it this way, **"For we walk by faith, not
by sight"** (2 Corinthians 5:7).

You see, every time we refuse to obey God, whether out of fear or self-preservation, we prove to God that we are not ready to go on to the next stage in His plan for us. No matter how reasonable our excuses seem for not obeying, we have to stay in His will in order to enjoy His blessings for our lives.

For instance, suppose God calls a person to the pastoral ministry and tells him to attend Bible school this year. But he decides not to go because he is afraid he may not make it through to graduation. He even feels he has several good reasons for not going.

Well, until that person does what God told him to do, he won't be ready to go on to the next step in God's plan for his life. He will have to obey God regarding Bible school or he will detour until God can get him into His will again.

In some things the window for opportunity to obey closes, and God has to chart a different path for you to get you into His perfect will. Other times, if you're in a place of struggle, look back to the last place where you didn't obey God. Repent and do what He told you to do. Get that right so that you can move ahead.

Your calling does not change. The callings of God are without repentance. For instance, if He called you to the healing ministry but you decided you didn't want to do that, God is still waiting for you to answer that divine call. The answer is simple. Just say, "Yes, Lord," and trust Him to show you the way.

When God called me to preach, I protested, "Lord, I can't do that. You know I can't stand on a platform and preach. You know I can't lay hands on the sick. I've never done that, and I don't *want* to do that!"

Well, do you know where I'd be spiritually if I had stayed in that unwilling state of heart? I'd be right at that place where I said, "Lord, I can't do that." I only moved on to the next level

in my walk with God when I made the decision to obey what I had heard!

In life you can make wrong choices and miss God. He will begin to maneuver you back into His plan. No matter how far you drift from God's plan, if you repent, He can always get you back and make it possible for you to live in His perfect plan. You can't unscramble eggs but God can!

LEARNING TO LIVE BY GOD'S WORDS

God proves us each step of the way to see if our hearts will remain obedient to Him, no matter how we feel or what circumstances we may face. We can find His purpose for proving us in Deuteronomy 8:3: **"that he might make thee know that man doth not live by bread only, but by every word that proceedeth out of the mouth of the Lord doth man live."** We have to learn to trust and obey *before* we meet the giants.

Notice we are to live by *every* word that proceeds out of the mouth of the Lord—not just our favorite words.

Why? Because in our born-again spirits, we want to know God's way. We want to know what He thinks about things so that our minds can be renewed to agree with Him. We want to flow *with* Him and not *against* Him. The more our souls are renewed to accept as truth what God says about any subject, the freer we are, and the harder it is for the devil to get a foothold in our lives.

We don't know nearly enough. But, thank God, we know enough to live free! And we're always in the process of learning more. If we are moving on with God, we are continually hearing more and doing more of God's Word. We are asking for more revelation (wisdom and understanding). We want to live by every word that proceeds out of the mouth of God.

Living by *every* word includes accepting the Lord's words of discipline. Deuteronomy 8:5 says, **"Thou shalt also consider in thine heart, that, as a man chasteneth his son, so the Lord thy God chasteneth thee."** This scripture isn't talking about God inflicting sickness or disease on us. Fathers of our flesh correct us in the flesh but the Father of our spirit corrects us in the spirit and, according to Hebrews 12:10, for our profit that we might be partakers of His holiness. *(The Amplified Bible* says, **"He disciplines us for our certain good."***)* It's talking about God training and disciplining us by His Word. Hebrews 12:5 tells us not to despise the chastening of the Lord. *The Amplified Bible* says, **"Do not think lightly or scorn to submit to the correction and discipline of the Lord, nor lose courage and give up and faint when you are reproved or corrected by Him."**

The word *chastise* means "to discipline, correct, instruct or train." The *Vine's Expository Dictionary of Biblical Words* says this word "primarily denotes 'to train children,' suggesting the broad idea of education."[1]

It's important to know that God's perfect plan for Israel was to go up armed and take possession of what He had given them. The wilderness experience came because they refused to trust and obey His plan.

A GOOD LAND WITHOUT SCARCENESS

God surely made great effort to get His people to hear and do, didn't He? That's how much He wanted to bring them into the good land He had provided for them. Just look at how good that land really was:

---

[1] W. E. Vine, *Vine's Expository Dictionary of Biblical Words* (Nashville: Thomas Nelson Publishers, 1985), p. 97.

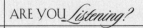

> For the Lord thy God bringeth thee into a good
> land, a land of brooks of water, of fountains and
> depths that spring out of valleys and hills; A land
> of wheat, and barley, and vines, and fig trees, and
> pomegranates; a land of oil olive, and honey.
>
> (Deuteronomy 8:7-8)

Do you recall the word used in the Bible to describe the
Garden of Eden which God prepared for His first man and
woman? *Good.* Genesis 1 says over and over, "God did this, and
it was *good.* God did that, and it was *good."* According to Genesis
1:31 it was *very* good. **"And God saw every thing that He had
made, and, behold, it was very good...."**

Here is the same Father, still endeavoring to get His people to
hear what He says and then to do it—so He can do them *good!*
He wants to give them the good land that He has prepared for
them, and lead them to victory over every enemy.

Now let's see what else God says through Moses about this
good land He has given Israel:

> **A land wherein thou shalt eat bread without
> scarceness, *thou shalt not lack any thing in it;* a land
> whose stones are iron, and out of whose hills thou
> mayest dig brass.**
>
> **(Deuteronomy 8:9)**

Can you imagine such a land? I mean, we have a better
covenant than the Israelites had, but this one would do pretty
well right now!

"Thou shalt not lack any thing in it." This is God's will for
His people. He *has* never changed. He *will* never change. Freedom

from lack is the way heaven has always operated, and the way it will continue to operate throughout eternity. That is also the way God's family can live if they will cleave unto Him and faithfully do what He says.

You have a heart to cleave to God if you are born again. God gave you that new heart in the new birth, and now you absolutely can obey God and do what He says about everything in your life. You can put yourself in a position to live without lack—of anything.

Now, if you're not interested in that kind of life, then don't do what God says. Just keep on doing whatever you are doing that keeps you struggling just to make it in life.

Personally, I got tired of struggling. I had tried it for a long time just because I didn't know any better. I didn't know there was another way to live.

But when Ken and I began to find out what was in the Word of God, we had no allegiance at all to that old, defeated lifestyle. We wanted out of debt! We were tired of being the tail. We were tired of wearing shoes with holes in them and never having enough to meet our basic needs.

So we turned to the Word of God. And as all the years have come and gone, God has never failed. Everything we ever lacked, He has provided. Every trial we ever faced, He has helped us to overcome. He has faithfully met every need.

GOD WANTS US FULL!

Deuteronomy 8:10 tells us the position in life God desires for His people: **"When thou hast eaten and art full, then thou shalt bless the Lord thy God for the good land which he hath given thee."**

God wants to give you the good of this life. It gives Him pleasure to see you prosper and experience fullness in every area of life (Psalm 35:27).

God has always wanted to have a people who know Him well and honor Him with their obedience, so He can take pleasure in freely blessing them in all things.

In fact, if God's perfect will were done in every one of our lives, we would all be full to overflowing, abounding in every good work. Second Corinthians 9:8 says it is God's desire that we have **"all sufficiency in all things."** *The Amplified Bible* says:

> **And God is able to make all grace (every favor and earthly blessing) come to you in abundance, so that you may always and under all circumstances and whatever the need be self-sufficient [possessing enough to require no aid or support and furnished in abundance for every good work and charitable donation].**
>
> **(2 Corinthians 9:8)**

That's a New Testament witness to the fact that God wants us to enjoy the fullness of His blessings, and yet, God wants your heart. He wants you to follow Him and do His Word, to put Him first and honor Him above all else. That is the prerequisite for receiving **"the good land which he hath given thee."** Your loyalty to Him opens wide the door of blessing.

REJOICING IN GOD'S GOODNESS

Do you know what really pleases God? He likes it when every one of our needs is met so that when we come into His presence, we don't have to spend a lot of time talking to Him about our rent payment or our car bills. We can just rejoice in His goodness.

God likes rejoicing, but most of the time He hears only petitions, such as "God, I've got to have my rent by the fifteenth of the month!" Yet, right here in Deuteronomy, He has written down the answer to our rent and to any other need we might have. We just have to hear and do it.

Deuteronomy 8:10 tells us what we should do—we should bless the Lord for His goodness! Every day we ought to go before the Lord and thank Him: "Lord, I just want to thank You for all the good You are doing for me and for my family. Thank You, Lord, for Your provision. Thank You for the good Word that You reveal to us!" That's called blessing the Lord!

God wants His people to enjoy life. And, this may shock you, but the truth is that *God* enjoys life! The Bible says that in His presence is *fullness of joy* (Psalm 16:11).

Real joy comes only from the manifestation of God in our lives. The more of God's presence we enjoy in this life, the more wonderful our lives are!

DON'T FORGET GOD

After telling us what we should do when we receive His blessings, God warns us about what we should not do:

> Beware that *thou forget not the Lord thy God*, in not keeping his commandments, and his judgments, and his statutes, which I command thee this day: Lest when thou hast eaten and art full, and hast built goodly houses, and dwelt therein; And when thy herds and thy flocks multiply, and thy silver and thy gold is multiplied, and all that thou hast is multiplied; Then thine heart be lifted up, and thou forget the Lord thy God,

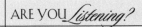

which brought thee forth out of the land of Egypt,
from the house of bondage.

(Deuteronomy 8:11-14)

God wants you to hear and obey Him so you can be blessed
and dwell in goodly houses full of good things. But God also
warns you not to forget Him in the process.

Instead, verse 18 tells us that we are to remember the Lord as
the One Who gives us the power, or the ability, to get wealth:

But thou shalt remember the Lord thy God: for it is
he that giveth thee power to get wealth, that he may
establish his covenant which he sware unto thy fathers,
as it is this day.

There is an anointing to get wealth. It isn't some kind of evil
anointing; it comes from God.

Moses is telling Israel on God's behalf, "When you begin to
increase in every area of your life, remember Who gave you the
increase. Don't forget to keep hearing and doing, because wealth
can go a lot quicker than it comes. The only way to secure your
wealth is to continue to hear and obey God in what He says." Or
you could say it like this, "Keep God first place in your life."

Of course, once you are entrenched in this lifestyle of obedience to God, everything else pales in comparison. You aren't
interested in sin any longer. Sitting in some dark, dirty bar drink-
ing alcohol is no temptation to you after you have tasted true
life. All you want to do is come to a Believers' Convention and
hear someone preach more of God's Word to you! Our joy and
pleasure are in our Father.

LET GOD ESTABLISH HIS COVENANT IN YOUR LIFE

Many times we think about prosperity as something we are trying to get God to do for us. But, really, God has been trying to get us to let Him prosper us so that He can establish the covenant He has already sworn and promised.

Notice in verse 18 that God's purpose in giving us the power to get wealth is **"that he may establish his covenant which he sware unto thy fathers, as it is this day."** Have you ever thought about how important it is to God that we let Him establish His covenant in our lives? God wanted that so badly that He swore by Himself, promising Abraham, **"I will bless you…and you will be a blessing"** (Genesis 12:2, AMP).

Prosperity is not man's idea. God *wants* us to prosper. So why should we insult Him by hindering Him from fulfilling His covenant with us by holding out in unbelief or disobedience?

It is also important to understand that prosperity is progressive. When Ken and I first entered the ministry, we thought, *If God would give us $100 million, we'd know just what to do with it!*

But the truth is that we weren't really ready for $100 million back then, and God knew it. He knew we had to grow into that kind of responsibility.

So, all through these years Kenneth and I have increased and increased and increased. Some years we would stay about the same, but then we'd begin to increase again. Now we're able to believe for that level of finances to come in. We need that much and more to fulfill what God has called us to do in this hour!

GOD WANTS YOUR HEART BEFORE HE GIVES YOU WEALTH

God wants to prosper you, so He won't give you something that will hurt you. He has to have your heart before He can give you wealth.

You see, you can't stay out of the will of God and still prosper. You may make money, but you can't prosper.

There are wicked people in this world who are rich, but they aren't prospering. Often, the more money they make, the quicker they die. Why? Because they buy all the drugs and immorality they want until they finally kill themselves!

Even if those who are rich live long lives, they have no peace without God. And living a long life with a lot of money but no peace is *not* God's idea of prosperity!

So God will prove you to see what you will do with His Word in the circumstances of life. He wants to know whether or not He will remain in first place in your life after He has blessed you with material increase.

That's why you have to stay sharp spiritually, stay in the Word and walk circumspectly before God. Every time you pass a test, you qualify for increase!

Prayer of Consecration

Lord, I'm willing to do what You have called me to do. I know that if You tell me to do it, You will enable me to do it. You will make the way straight and part the Red Sea if necessary!

I believe for the power to get wealth so You can establish Your covenant in my life. I promise that I will always remember where my increase came from. No matter what, I will stay true to You!

THINK ON THESE THINGS

*God wants to be the Light that overwhelms the
darkness in every area of our lives until
we are blessed above all people!*

*We are to live by every word that proceeds out of
the mouth of the Lord—not just our favorite words.*

CHAPTER 6

ENJOYING DAYS
OF HEAVEN
ON EARTH

W e're still making our way through Deuteronomy, stopping here and there to see the many ways God tells Israel to hearken to His Word. God is trying His best to get something over to His people. He knows that their lives depend on it. So over and over, He keeps saying the same thing in different ways.

WHAT DOES GOD REQUIRE OF US?

In Deuteronomy 10:12-13, Moses tells the Israelites what God requires of them. Nothing has changed since the day Moses first spoke these words. God requires the same thing of us today.

> **And now, Israel, what doth the Lord thy God require of thee, but to fear the Lord thy God, to walk in all his ways, and to love him, and to serve the Lord thy God with all thy heart and with all thy soul, To keep the commandments of the Lord, and his statutes, which I command thee this day for thy good?**

What does the Lord require of us? To fear Him. To honor Him. To reverence Him. To let Him be God. To walk in His ways.

To love and to serve Him. To keep His Word. To always be available to serve Him with all our hearts and souls.

That's what God asked His people to do. That's the foundation of Bible prosperity. In return, He would do them good. They would experience blessing and continual increase in every area.

Deuteronomy 11:8 tells us why all these blessings result from our obedience to God: **"Therefore shall ye keep all the commandments which I command you this day, that ye may be strong, and go in and possess the land, whither ye go to possess it."**

Keeping God's commandments makes us strong, because our obedience enables God to move into our lives with His power. Obedience also keeps prosperity from hurting us. You see, prosperity only ruins fools, and when we listen to God, we are not fools.

Verse 18 goes on to say, **"Therefore shall ye lay up these my words in your heart and in your soul, and bind them for a sign upon your hand, that they may be as frontlets between your eyes."**

God's Word was the key to Israel's existence. It was the key to their success in life. They had to lay up His words in their hearts so they wouldn't forget them. Only God's Word could help them walk the straight path of obedience without turning to the right or to the left. Only the Word could make them strong so that they could do what God required of them.

DAYS OF HEAVEN ON EARTH

Deuteronomy 11:21-24a gives us another glimpse into what God planned for His people in the good land He had prepared:

That your days may be multiplied, and the days of your children, in the land which the Lord sware unto your fathers to give them, as the days of heaven upon the earth.

For if ye shall diligently keep all these commandments which I command you, to do them, to love the Lord your God, to walk in all his ways, and to cleave unto him;

Then will the Lord drive out all these nations from before you, and ye shall possess greater nations and mightier than yourselves. Every place whereon the soles of your feet shall tread shall be yours.

What did God want for His people? Lack, turmoil, defeat? No! He wanted them to have the best of everything. He wanted their crops to be abundant and their homes to be fine. He wanted them to enjoy days of heaven on earth.

What does that mean? Well, during days of heaven on earth, everything is done just as it is in heaven. It's done correctly in heaven. It's done *big* in heaven. Everything is perfect in heaven. There is no lack. Heaven's citizens don't even know what lack is!

Days of heaven on earth include the ability to drive out enemies that are "mightier than ourselves." You see, that's why we can't look at natural circumstances to see what God can do in our lives. We're not dealing with the natural realm; therefore, we have to look past those circumstances and into the Word to see what God says.

Days of heaven on the earth! Days of supernatural provision on the earth! Days of increase on the earth! All this awaits us when we honor God and keep His ways. God has always wanted a people who would hear and do what He says, so He could manifest Himself and give us days of heaven on earth.

That was the essence of Jesus' message when He went around preaching and teaching the kingdom of God. Jesus would say, **"The kingdom of God is come nigh unto you"** (Luke 10:9). In other words, He was saying, "It's here right now. You can be healed and delivered right now because the kingdom, or the dominion, of God is here."

Jesus manifested the kingdom of God wherever He went. Death had to bow its knee. Devils had to run. Sickness had to flee. The things of this earth, such as loaves and fishes being multiplied, had to respond to His blessing.

Well, our citizenship is in the kingdom of God. We are citizens of heaven, ambassadors representing the Lord Jesus Christ on this earth until Jesus returns.

I don't know how much longer that will be. But however long it is, I am going to be one of those who continues to diligently hearken to the Lord so I can enjoy days of heaven on earth!

"ALL THESE BLESSINGS SHALL COME ON THEE"

Let's skip ahead to Deuteronomy 28, the chapter that lists both the blessings and the curses of the Law. I want to show you that God has always given His people the choice of whether or not to hearken to His Word.

> **And it shall come to pass, if thou shalt hearken diligently unto the voice of the Lord thy God, to observe and to do all his commandments which I command thee this day, that the Lord thy God will set thee on high above all nations of the earth: And all**

these blessings shall come on thee, and overtake thee, if thou shalt hearken unto the voice of the Lord thy God.

(Deuteronomy 28:1-2)

Notice how this chapter starts out: When the Bible uses the word *shall*, it should be interpreted as "inevitable, unavoidable or predetermined." In other words, "It is inevitable—all My blessings *shall* come on you *if* you will hearken to My Word." This will come to pass.

All of God's blessings! The children of Israel could expect some heavy-duty blessings to come their way if they walked in obedience! Just take the time to read verses 3-14, and you will see what I mean.

Everything you can think of is included in those blessings. When you hearken unto God, you will be blessed in the city, blessed in the field, blessed coming in and blessed going out. You will have a surplus of prosperity. You will be blessed in the fruit of your body and the fruit of your cattle. Your storage places (plural!) will be filled with plenty. Everything you put your hand to will prosper. You will enjoy blessing, increase and abundance in every area of your life—days of heaven on earth!

Jesus said something very similar in Matthew 6:33. Basically, He said, "Seek God first and His way of doing and being right. And as you put God first, all of His blessings will be added unto you."

One of the end results God sought to accomplish in blessing His people with days of heaven on earth is found in Deuteronomy 28:10: **"All people of the earth shall see that thou art called by the name of the Lord; and they shall be afraid of thee."**

This verse reminds me of testimonies I've heard from people who know how to give and to walk in prosperity. For instance, one minister said that over a period of time, he just kept getting blessed with cars and boats that he parked around his home.

Finally, his neighbor came over and asked, "What are you doing? Setting up a car lot or something?"

"No, I'm just enjoying the blessings of the Lord!" the minister exclaimed.

People ought to be able to see the blessing of God on our lives. After all, we represent God to the world.

Now, don't be like some people and say, "Well, you know, I'm a preacher. I have to look good, so I'll go down and borrow the money to buy me a Mercedes Benz." Well, you won't look good when the creditors come looking for you to pay for that Benz!

Let your prosperity come naturally. Let God bless you. Maintaining an image isn't the issue here. Image doesn't mean much if it doesn't reflect reality. When you have to *try* to look good, you are actually putting on a facade and not conveying a true image.

Also, don't start thinking, *Oh, I feel kind of depressed today. I think I'll just go down and buy me a new suit. I really can't afford it, but it will make me feel better.* That isn't a cure for depression. You'll get a big bill at the end of the month and have no money to pay it. Then you *will* have a reason to be depressed!

Remember, God wants to bless you above all people. He wants you to enjoy days of heaven on this earth. You don't have to run after blessings. Just get in line with God's Word, and His blessings will run after you!

BLESSINGS OR CURSES?

Later in Deuteronomy 28, God gives "the other side of the coin"—the consequences of choosing not to hearken. Verse 15 says:

But it shall come to pass, if thou wilt not hearken unto the voice of the Lord thy God, to observe to do all his commandments and his statutes which I command thee this day; that all these curses shall come upon thee, and overtake thee.

If Israel hearkened unto God, all of His blessings would come upon them. If they chose not to hearken, they would suffer the consequences.

You see, you have to read the *ifs* in the Bible. You receive the blessings only after you fulfill the *ifs*.

In Deuteronomy 30:19, Moses set forth the choice Israel had to make:

I call heaven and earth to record this day against you, that I have set before you life and death, blessing and cursing: therefore choose life, that both thou and thy seed may live.

It was up to the children of Israel. They had to choose. They could either be blessed, or they could be cursed. But if they wanted life and blessing, instead of death and cursing, they had to choose God and His ways.

You just can't choose God without choosing His ways. It is the choosing of His ways that makes life a blessing on this earth. When you don't choose God's ways, you are actually choosing darkness, defeat, lack, sickness—the entire curse of the Law.

Deuteronomy 28:15-68 defines all the curses the children of Israel subjected themselves to through disobedience—and believe me, there are plenty of curses out there in the world to choose from! Every sickness and disease is under that curse.

Losing one's children is under that curse. Fear, doubt, anguish and oppression are all under that curse.

Thank God, Jesus redeemed us from the curse so we could live and walk in God's blessings (Galatians 3:13-14)! But the ability to enjoy His blessings still hinges on whether or not we honor God with our obedience. Even though we have a better covenant, we can't make new-covenant blessings come to pass in our lives without being obedient to God.

"But I don't want to tithe." Well, that's your choice. You just decided not to do it God's way. "I don't want to spend time in the Word." Again, that's your choice. You just decided to miss out on the one thing that causes you to become victorious in this life: fellowshiping with God in His Word. "I don't want to pray." Once again, you just decided to miss out on the very thing that puts you in contact with God so you can be led by His Spirit.

If God has called you into the ministry, you may be saying, "But I don't want to preach." Well, you're doing the same thing Israel did—rebelling against the call of God. What will happen as long as you do that? Very little good in your life. You are blessed only when you are in the will of God, hearing and obeying Him. That's always the bottom line.

"HARDEN NOT YOUR HEARTS"

Over and over, God promised Israel that if they would obey Him, no enemy could stand before them—nothing could defeat them. Yet an entire generation of Israelites failed to enter the Promised Land that God had given them. It wasn't God's fault; they had made their choice.

Let's look in Hebrews 3 to find out more about what happened and why. We can learn a lesson for our own lives from Israel's failure to inherit the blessings of their covenant with God.

> **Wherefore (as the Holy Ghost saith, Today if ye will hear his voice, Harden not your hearts, as in the provocation, in the day of temptation in the wilderness: When your fathers tempted me, proved me, and saw my works forty years. Wherefore I was grieved with that generation, and said, *They do always err in their heart; and they have not known my ways...*).**
>
> **(Hebrews 3:7-10)**

These verses explain why that generation couldn't enter the Promised Land. They hadn't given God their hearts. They weren't loyal to Him. They didn't do what He said. They did not know His ways.

Over and over, God had revealed Himself, manifested Himself and proven Himself to His people. They had seen all the plagues that came upon Egypt. They had seen it become so dark in Egypt that no man moved for three days, yet there had been light in the land of Goshen. They had seen all the firstborn of Egypt die, yet not one of their own firstborn had been harmed. They had even seen the Red Sea stand up like two walls of jello as they walked across on dry ground! The Israelites had seen all these signs and wonders, yet they still wouldn't do what God said, and He was grieved with them.

Verses 7-8 say, **"Today if ye will hear his voice, Harden not your hearts."** That's the key. Unbelief had hardened the people's hearts, so they couldn't enter in.

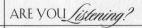
Hebrews 4:2 goes on to say that the words God spoke to them didn't do them any good because they didn't mix faith with what they heard. They refused to receive what God spoke into their hearts—to let it abide there and bear fruit. They rejected it, saying, "We can't," even though God had told them, "You can!"

Now, that is *not* the way you receive the Word. When you hear the Word preached or when you see a truth in the Bible, you are to say, "Lord, I receive that! I believe it because it's in Your Word. I'm asking You for more wisdom on this, but I'm telling You right now—I believe it!"

Out of that entire generation, only Joshua and Caleb received God's words with that kind of simple faith. And to those two men, God said, "I'm going to give you the land." And He did exactly that!

GROWING IN OBEDIENCE TO GOD

Ever since Ken and I first found out the truth about the Word of God—that we could depend on it, that it was our written covenant with God—we've been working on obeying everything it says. That was the difference between us and a lot of other people back in the early days. Others heard the same thing we did but didn't do anything with it. They didn't mix faith with what they heard. No one knows where those people are today!

Ken and I were just little nobodies in Kenneth Hagin's early Tulsa meetings. We were glad to be able to get in the door! But even though we were new to the message of faith, we had the hearts of a Joshua and a Caleb. We were ready to act on every new truth we learned from God's Word!

By then, Brother Hagin had been in the ministry for more than 30 years. Ken and I decided to take what he had learned during those three decades, plant it in our hearts, put it in our mouths and apply it to our lives. We weren't looking for our own message. We didn't want to start over when it was possible to learn from someone who was already walking in faith. Why should we struggle trying to figure out for ourselves what we could learn from his many years of experience? That is why God sets teachers in the Church—so we can learn from them and every generation doesn't have to start at zero.

That willingness to learn from those who were more experienced in this faith walk put Ken and me ahead. Within a few months of listening to Brother Hagin's tapes and sermons, Ken was out preaching what he had learned from him. And from those small beginnings, our ministry continues to increase.

Through the years, our capacity to be obedient to the Word has continued to grow. We haven't reached perfection by any means, but we've come a long way from where we were! And the thing that changed our lives the most was our decision to simply honor the Word as if it were God speaking directly to us. That's all God ever asked of us. That's all He ever asks of anyone.

CHOOSE LIFE!

Israel had a decision to make: life or death, blessing or cursing. Cursing was automatic for them if they didn't hearken to God; blessings were inevitable if they did hear and obey.

The same is true for us today. We must choose whether or not we will hearken to God's Word. If we hearken to God regarding the new birth, then we are born again. If we hearken to God and do what He says about healing, then healing takes place in our lives. If we hearken to His Word regarding prosperity, then we begin to prosper. In every area, if we will just obey God and walk in His light, we will automatically increase in His life and blessings.

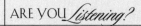

I don't know about you, but I choose life! Every time I choose to obey the written Word of God, I choose life. Every time I choose to obey God in my spirit when He tells me to do something, I choose life.

How do *you* choose life? You just have to decide, "I'm staying with the Word of God. As I hear and obey what God says, I believe it is unavoidable and predetermined that God's blessings will overtake me. I will have the things I need. In fact, I'll even have a surplus of prosperity! It is inevitable. It shall come to pass!"

Then determine never to quit. Don't let yourself think, *Well, that will never work for me,* or *They prayed for me, but I didn't get healed.*

As faith men and women, we can never quit. We must not reach this great moment in the history of the Church, only to draw back in fear! No, this is the time to *double up,* not give up!

So prove yourself faithful in the hard places. Keep honoring God with your mouth. Keep putting the Word into your heart so you will be able to accomplish all that God has placed in your heart to do.

The key to Israel's deliverance was to hearken unto God. We hold that same key. As we hear and do the Word of God, certain victory and days of heaven on earth will be ours!

Prayer of Consecration

Lord, I set myself to honor You above all things, circumstances, people or opinions that are in the earth. I give You my allegiance. I'm here for You. I'll do whatever You want me to do. Should Jesus return in my generation, I want Him to find me in trust and obedience, nothing doubting!

THINK ON THESE THINGS

*Keeping God's commandments makes us strong because
our obedience enables God to move into our lives with His power.*

*Days of supernatural provision on the earth!
Days of increase on the earth! All this awaits us
when we honor God and keep His ways.*

*You have to read the ifs in the Bible. You receive
the blessings only after you fulfill the ifs.*

*We must not reach this great moment in the
history of the Church, only to draw back in fear!
No, this is the time to double up, not give up!*

CHAPTER 7

The book of Jeremiah provides another clear and accurate picture of God's history with His people. In this book, we can once again see how God gave them the same message over and over and over again. The Scripture says He continually sent prophets to them—men of God who rose early on a daily basis to go tell His people what they should do for their own good (Jeremiah 7:25, 35:15). Yet, again and again, the people refused to hearken to what God said through those He sent.

We can recognize this same pattern even in our own Christian experience. All we have to do is think of the times in our lives when we learned more revelation and then faced the choice of whether to receive or reject it. And we shouldn't deceive ourselves into thinking we received that revelation if we didn't act on it. Just because we mentally agree with the Bible does not mean we are hearing it with the intent to *do* it. Our victory is in the follow-through.

Taking the Word into your heart means letting it abide there. John 15:7 is one of the most important revelations in the Bible: **"If ye abide in me, and my words abide in you, ye shall ask what ye will, and it shall be done unto you."** The Word that is abiding in you is the Word that talks to you. It comes out of your

mouth continually. It becomes your reality and defines your response to situations you face.

This is what the people of Judah failed to do, and they eventually went into captivity. Let's learn from their mistakes so we can avoid the same fate!

THE FAITHFULNESS OF JEREMIAH

As I studied the life and ministry of the prophet Jeremiah, it struck me to see how faithful to God he was. Even when it threatened to cost his freedom or his life, Jeremiah kept doing what God told him to do. He kept preaching the same sermon, year after year after year. The people wouldn't listen to him, but still Jeremiah continued. He wouldn't quit. He was faithful.

You know, you can't always tell whether you're in the will of God by the way people respond to you. You may think, *I just can't seem to get my ministry going. Maybe God never called me in the first place.* Well, you need to remember that it's really not *your* ministry. It's the Lord's work on the earth, and He may have deliberately led you to a place where you have to deal with some hardheaded people because He needed you there, just as He did Jeremiah.

If Jeremiah had used the people's responses to his message as his gauge for success, he would have given up in the first year of ministry! The people ridiculed him, cast him into a dungeon and even tried to kill him. But they couldn't stop Jeremiah. He had a one-track mind; he was determined to say whatever God told him, even if the message sounded repetitive and was rejected by the people who heard it.

ANSWER YOUR CALL

Let's look at what God said to Jeremiah when He called him as a prophet to Judah:

Before I formed thee in the belly I knew thee; and before thou camest forth out of the womb I sanctified thee, and I ordained thee a prophet unto the nations.

(Jeremiah 1:5)

Listen, if you know that you have a call to the ministry on your life, now is the time to step out and answer that call. You may think, *I know I'm called, but I just can't see myself in the ministry. I'm just not capable of such a thing!*

Jeremiah had those same kinds of reservations. He said, **"Ah, Lord God! behold, I cannot speak: for I am a child"** (v. 6).

But the Lord had an answer for Jeremiah's protests:

Say not, I am a child: for thou shalt go to all that I shall send thee, and whatsoever I command thee thou shalt speak. Be not afraid of their faces: for I am with thee to deliver thee, saith the Lord.

(Jeremiah 1:7-8)

Check out all the different people in the Bible (Moses, Gideon, etc.) who protested the call of God because they didn't think they were capable of fulfilling it. You'll find that God always answered their protests the same way: "I am with you."

For instance, Moses asked, "Who am I to go to Pharaoh?" God responded, "Certainly I will go with you" (Exodus 3:11-12). In other words, "Moses, who you are is not important here. It is *Who is with you* that is important."

That's still true today. Who we are is not important. When it comes to answering God's call, the important consideration is *Who is with us.* In ourselves, we could never fulfill the work of God. But we can obey what God tells us to do and then let *Him* do His part—the impossible, supernatural part.

Our part is revealed in God's words to Jeremiah in verse 9: **"Behold, I have put my words in thy mouth."** Don't tell me that the words of your mouth are not important! I've read too much Bible to believe that. The importance of the words you speak is written throughout the Bible. You are to speak the words that *God* puts in your heart.

Then the Lord said something remarkable to Jeremiah:

> **See, I have this day set thee over the nations and over the kingdoms, to root out, and to pull down, and to destroy, and to throw down, to build, and to plant.**
>
> **(Jeremiah 1:10)**

Isn't that amazing? God told Jeremiah, "I've set you over nations." Just one man! I'm telling you, *one person who follows God can make a difference in the outcome of this whole world!*

Think about Noah. He was the only righteous man left on the face of the earth. What if he had turned God down when He told him to build an ark? Noah could have rejected that command, and the outcome of the entire human race would have been forever affected. But, thank God, Noah chose to hear and do!

I don't know what God has called you to do. But I guarantee you, there is a niche in His plans that He is depending on you to fill for Him. It doesn't matter who you are, where you came from or how smart you are. What matters is that you will hear and do what He says. As you obey God, He will work through you to bring about whatever He desires.

On the other hand, if you refuse to answer God's call, you will continue to live in bondage. That's just the way it is. There are no exceptions.

In Jeremiah 7:13, God told the people of Judah, **"I called you, but ye answered not."** You don't ever want to be guilty of that offense. The moment God calls you and you refuse to answer, you are already in trouble because God knows what is best for you. His way may not be easy, but it is always good; it is always rewarding. His way is life. The more you follow God's plan for your life, the more you really live.

THE BOUNDLESS MERCY OF GOD

I'm going to show you some scriptures throughout the book of Jeremiah that prove God's message to the people of Judah never changed. He just kept telling them the same thing: They had to hear and do His Word to be blessed. He never gave a substitute formula for that simple principle.

I also want you to see how faithful and merciful God was to help His people, even though they continued to turn Him down. Jeremiah 3:11-14 shows His heart toward Israel:

> **And the Lord said unto me, The backsliding Israel hath justified herself more than treacherous Judah.**
>
> **Go and proclaim these words toward the north, and say, Return, thou backsliding Israel, saith the Lord; and I will not cause mine anger to fall upon you: for I am merciful, saith the Lord, and I will not keep anger for ever.**

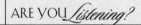
> Only acknowledge thine iniquity, that thou hast
> transgressed against the Lord thy God, and hast
> scattered thy ways to the strangers under every green
> tree, and ye have not obeyed my voice, saith the Lord.
> Turn, O backsliding children, saith the Lord; for I am
> married unto you.

Isn't that something? God looked at His covenant with Judah as a marriage covenant. He said, "I am married to you." He wouldn't give up on them, just like He won't give up on you and me.

Many times God told His people through Jeremiah that certain calamities would come to pass if they didn't change. But then, almost in the next breath, He promised that a day would come when He would gather them again unto Himself. Now that's the mercy of God!

The devil may be telling you that you've gone too far astray for too long. You may think you have refused God's call past the point of no return, and now it's too late to answer it.

But it's never too late! If you will repent, you can get back. God sent the prophet Jeremiah to tell His people His will for their lives. Jeremiah's ministry lasted about 40 years, extending through the regime of several kings. And throughout those four decades, God spoke the same message through him to Judah. God never gave up on His people. He just kept endeavoring to get them to repent so He could have mercy on them and avert the evil that was in their future unless they turned from their way to God's way.

God's mercy toward His people is boundless. The Bible says that God's mercy endures forever and that He delights in mercy (Psalm 106:1; Micah 7:18).

Jeremiah went on to say in Lamentations 3:23 that God's mercies are new every morning. Now think about that verse in connection with Jeremiah 7:25. God said, **"Since the day that your fathers came forth out of the land of Egypt unto this day I have even sent unto you all my servants the prophets, daily rising up early and sending them."** In other words, every morning God sent prophets to Israel to tell them what they ought to do in order to avoid defeat, year after year after year. It's amazing to see how much God cared for Israel. And He still cares that much for us today!

I'm telling you, God is a good God! F.F. Bosworth said this of the Lord's compassion:

> Suppose the vast Pacific [O]cean were elevated high above us. Then conceive of its pressure into every crevice to find an outlet through which it might pour its ocean-tides over all the earth, and you have a picture of God's benevolent attitude toward us.
>
> After being first properly enlightened, I challenge you, Reader, to place yourself where God's mercy can reach you without His having to violate the glorious principles of His moral government, then wait and see if you don't experience the most overwhelming demonstration of His love and mercy, and the blessing will flow until you have reached the limit of your expectation.[1]

That's what the Word does for us: It helps us to place ourselves where God's mercy can reach us "without His having to violate the glorious principles of His moral government." When God teaches us His ways, He enables us to keep ourselves in a position to receive from Him as we walk in His ways.

---

[1] F.F. Bosworth, *Christ the Healer* (Grand Rapids, Michigan: Fleming H. Revell, 1973), p. 65.

God's mercies are new every morning. I don't care how exasperating we are to Him, we cannot wear out His mercy!

THE KEY TO INCREASE

Jeremiah 3:15 tells us one of the things God promised to do for His people in His mercy: **"And I will give you pastors according to mine heart, which shall feed you with knowledge and understanding."**

The key to the people's success was obtaining God's knowledge and understanding. As they walked in His wisdom, they couldn't help but increase, as the next verse states: **"And it shall come to pass, when ye be multiplied and increased in the land..."** (v. 16).

On the other hand, Jeremiah 5:25 tells us what happens when we don't walk in God's wisdom: **"Your iniquities have turned away these things, and *your sins have withholden good things from you."*** This is a simple concept. You can't misunderstand it. If you do what is right, good things will come into your life. If you don't do what is right in God's sight, you don't qualify for the good.

I'm thoroughly convinced of this fact: When you open up your heart to God's wisdom and live every day with the intent to obey His Word, you will experience increase in your life. However, that doesn't mean you will go from being broke to enjoying abundance overnight. In Exodus 23:30, God tells the Israelites: **"By little and little I will drive them out from before thee, until thou be increased, and inherit the land."** That's the law of progressive increase.

I do believe that things have sped up in this hour, however. You certainly can increase more quickly than Ken and I were able to, because you can learn what the Lord has taught us for more than 32 years and grow quickly.

Increase for Ken and me began immediately, but six months later or even six years later we were definitely not where we are today. As we remained faithful to obey God over a period of months and years and decades, we have continued to steadily increase.

It works that way because revelation is progressive. You can't learn everything the first six weeks after you become a Christian. You gradually receive the blessings that belong to you as you keep hearing, believing and applying the Word to your life. How fast you learn depends on how diligent you are about the things of God.

Ken and I are still learning and still increasing. Meanwhile, I continually reflect on all the good that God has done in our lives over the past 32 years. I never want to forget those days when we had to believe God for money to buy groceries. I like to be reminded of the faithfulness of God! God admonishes us to REMEMBER where our blessings come from. **"But thou shalt remember the Lord thy God: for it is he that giveth thee power to get wealth, that he may establish his covenant which he sware unto thy fathers, as it is this day"** (Deuteronomy 8:18).

ALLOW GOD TO CORRECT YOU

Unfortunately, the people of Judah didn't remember those words and walk according to God's knowledge and understanding. God said, **"This people hath a revolting and a rebellious heart; they are revolted and gone"** (Jeremiah 5:23). They had wicked hearts. They wouldn't do what God said. They wouldn't allow Him to correct them.

We need to realize that every correction is a blessing from God. Titus 2:11-12 says that it is the grace and favor of God that teaches us to live godly in this present world.

So when God corrects you, don't get upset with Him. His kingdom can be manifested in your life only when you are obedient. God is trying to keep you in a position to be blessed. He wants to keep you in His will, because there is blessing only in the will of God. Outside of His will is struggle and turmoil and defeat.

You have to be willing to be corrected by the Word of God in order to increase supernaturally and to walk in peace. If you won't be corrected, then you aren't hearing God. And if you're not hearing God, He can't take His place in your life as Healer and Provider.

Remember, He has set before us a choice: Hearken to His Word, and all of His blessings will overtake us; refuse to hearken, and we open ourselves to the curse of the Law.

So let the Word correct you. I don't care what religious tradition you grew up with. Let go of the traditions you have heard all your life and find out what the Word really says. Jesus said that the traditions of men make the Word of God of no effect.

In the book of Jeremiah, we have a clear example of a people who refused to hearken to God or to be corrected by what His prophet had to say. Actually, it's an amazing eye-opener to read the book of Jeremiah and see just how bold the people were in their rebellion. For instance, look at Jeremiah 6:16:

> **Thus saith the Lord, Stand ye in the ways, and see, and ask for the old paths, where is the good way, and walk therein, and ye shall find rest for your souls. But they said, We will not walk therein.**

The people showed no fear and no honor of God. There is nothing God can do for people like that. He will not cross His Word. He gave them His Word and said, "If you go the way of disobedience, the curse will come on you" (Deuteronomy 28:15, author's paraphrase). It was a judgment they brought on themselves through their disobedience.

DON'T LET HIS WORD BE A REPROACH TO YOU

Jeremiah 6:10 even says that God's Word was a *reproach* to His people:

> **To whom shall I speak, and give warning, that they may hear? behold, their ear is uncircumcised, and they cannot hearken: behold, the word of the Lord is unto them a reproach; they have no delight in it.**

You know, many Christians get offended with different aspects of God's Word. For instance, it is a reproach to some people when they hear the Word concerning financial increase; they fight it with all they have. For others, it is a reproach to hear about God's will to heal them because it violates their traditions.

Back in the '40s and '50s, Oral Roberts came with a fresh revelation from God. God raised up Oral Roberts from the deathbed when he was a teenager. Then He sent him out preaching the revelation that God is a good God and He wants you well.

Preachers all over the nation, especially in his Pentecostal denomination, did not appreciate that good news at all. It was a reproach to them and their traditions. They wanted to kick him out for proclaiming the goodness of God!

Can you imagine being mad at someone because that person told you that God is a good God and that He wants you well?

Probably not. Well, the reason you find it so hard to imagine is that Oral Roberts stayed faithful to that message, despite the opposition of those who weren't glad to hear it. God also gave His own witness to the truth of that revelation by miraculously healing great multitudes of people. This simple message that God is a good God eventually changed the way a great portion of the Church looks at God's willingness to heal. What a wonderful revelation! God is a good God. Somebody had to proclaim it in power. Oral Roberts was faithful and obedient to answer God's call in spite of great opposition.

AMEND YOUR WAYS

We need to read Jeremiah as an admonition from the Lord teaching us not to disobey. It's no different for us than it was for the people of Judah. We *will* eat the fruit of our ways, but whether that fruit is good or bad depends on what we choose: to obey God or to rebel against Him.

If you are in trouble because of wrong choices, God has provided you with the solution in Jeremiah 7:3: **"Amend your ways and your doings."**

That's all it takes. God has given you the cure for faithlessness in this scripture: Find out what you're doing that isn't pleasing to God, and change it. Repent and come back to Him.

Now, Satan will try to tell you that God won't have you back, that you have gone too far. But that's a lie. Jesus is our advocate. His blood cleanses us of all sin. If we confess our sins, God is faithful and just to forgive us our sins (1 John 1:9).

So all through the book of Jeremiah, God says to Israel, as He still says to us, "Amend your ways, and turn back to Me."

"Oh, Gloria, I'd rather find an easier way. How about a prayer line?" No, that won't work forever. You can get help in a prayer line, but if you are walking contrary to God's ways, you won't be able to maintain that help. You have to amend your ways.

And you *can* amend your ways. Remember, the changes God requires of us in order to live in victory are do-able. He never asks us to do anything that is impossible. The impossible is His part. Our part is to follow His ways and to walk in the wisdom He so liberally offers.

Now, I want you to get a clear focus on God's will for Israel at this time. Was it His will that they be taken into captivity or that they amend their ways?

God told the people of Judah His will when He said, **"Amend your ways."** God's preference and desire for them was that they would walk with Him so that they could remain free. That's why He sent Jeremiah year after year after year with the same message.

God's will for you and me is the same as it was for Jeremiah's generation: that we would walk free of every yoke of bondage. But to live in that kind of freedom, we have to hear what God says and obey it!

Prayer of Consecration

Father, I give my all to You. I see the faithfulness and dedication of the prophet Jeremiah. I want You to know that I, too, will answer the call. Whatever You ask me to do, I'll do it! I yield to faithfulness, dedication and determination in the power of the Holy Spirit to be true to that commitment, and I will serve You the rest of my days on this earth.

<u>*THINK ON THESE THINGS*</u>

Taking the Word into your heart means letting it abide there.
The Word that is abiding in you is the Word that talks to you.
It comes out of your mouth continually.

One person who follows God can make a
difference in the outcome of this whole world!

The more you follow God's plan for your life, the more you really live.

When you open up your heart to God's wisdom and live every day with
the intent to obey His Word, you will experience increase in your life.

When God corrects you, don't get upset with Him. His kingdom
can be manifested in your life only when you are obedient.

CHAPTER 8

OBEY AND
BE BLESSED

As we work our way through the book of Jeremiah, a stop at Jeremiah 7:23 takes us back to the bottom line to victory that we read about time and time again in Deuteronomy. Once more, God reminds His people, **"Obey my voice, and I will be your God, and ye shall be my people: and** *walk ye in all the ways that I have commanded you, that it may be well unto you."*

We must walk in God's ways so that it may be well with us. That is a spiritual principle that never changes. It was true for Moses' generation, it remained true for Jeremiah's generation, and it still holds true today for our generation.

But as we have already seen, the people of Judah refused to hearken to God's admonition. Instead, they **"walked in the counsels and in the imagination of their evil heart, and went backward, and not forward"** (v. 24). As a result, it did not turn out well with them.

Now, if you want the formula for going backward in life, this verse gives it: Stop listening to God and begin to walk after the carnal imaginations of your heart. When you do that, you'll go backward. It's a formula that works every time. I don't recommend it, though. I strongly advise you to listen to God and go forward!

You can't be victorious in anything in this life unless God is right in the middle of it, and the only way to get Him involved is by hearing and obeying Him.

GOD WILL ALWAYS HAVE A WITNESS

"Obey and be blessed." Ever since God first delivered Israel out of Egypt, He continued to send His prophets to the people to deliver that central message. But, as Jeremiah 7:25-28 says:

> **Since the day that your fathers came forth out of the land of Egypt unto this day I have even sent unto you all my servants the prophets, daily rising up early and sending them: Yet they hearkened not unto me, nor inclined their ear, but hardened their neck: they did worse than their fathers.**
>
> **Therefore thou shalt speak all these words unto them; but they will not hearken to thee: thou shalt also call unto them; but they will not answer thee. But thou shalt say unto them, This is a nation that obeyeth not the voice of the Lord their God, nor receiveth correction: truth is perished, and is cut off from their mouth.**

This scripture confirmed something about the character of God that I had already learned. I saw that God kept sending prophets daily to His people, *knowing that the people would not listen.* That's how good God is!

God will always give a witness to every generation, even if He knows the people will not hear Him. He will not be guilty of having blood on His hands when the end comes. He sends people His Word, and they make their own choices whether to receive or reject it.

You see, God isn't looking for a way to keep people out of His family. He's trying to get more covenant people into His family. He wants more people who are born of Him—more sons and daughters. He told Abraham that all families of the earth would be blessed in him. God desires to give His witness to every nation and individual in this generation.

That thrills me. When I think of how faithful God was to give His witness to Israel and how much He has wanted to do good to His people in every generation, it makes it easy for me to believe that God will have compassion on me when I'm in trouble. That is just the way He is. He is full of mercy and goodness.

God had to have a witness, so Jeremiah kept prophesying the same thing to his hostile countrymen for 40 years. God will always do His part because of His great mercy, and one aspect of His part is to give people an opportunity to hear and obey.

The patience of God is so unfathomable. All He wanted was to be God in His people's lives. "Just let Me speak to you," He told them. "Let Me make your path straight. Let Me tell you what to do, and it will be well with you. You'll be blessed in your doing. You'll increase. Your seed will be blessed."

But the people of Judah said, "No, we don't want to do it that way, God."

And people are still saying that. "No, Lord, I just don't see how I can do what You're telling me to do." When someone says that, he is hardening his heart. He is refusing God, and trouble is coming. That person won't be able to avoid the consequences of disobedience, because when God speaks, His words never fail to come to pass.

As believers, we are God's witnesses on the earth today. We are to proclaim the good news to those in the world who live under the curse. It is our responsibility to tell them, "The kingdom of heaven is here. You can live in it. You can operate in it. Jesus paid the price for you. He redeemed you from the curse of poverty, sickness and spiritual death. You can be delivered out of darkness into the light of His abundant life!"

Now, the people we talk to can either take the truth or leave it. But that doesn't change our responsibility to proclaim the gospel. We have to be willing to keep on proclaiming, even if no one receives what we're saying. That's a lesson we learned from Jeremiah—and he lived in a day when people received God's words much less easily than they do today!

If the people receive the truth and act on it, faith comes into their hearts and they are immediately translated out of darkness into light. Then it's up to them to find out what belongs to them and begin to act on it so they can grow up and become strong in the Lord.

God told Ken and me to start a daily television broadcast in 1988. At the time, we were about a million dollars behind on the *Sunday* broadcast. Going on a *daily* broadcast didn't seem like a good solution to that problem! But God's leading was so strong that we did it anyway.

We certainly weren't looking for anything else to do. But God told us to get on television daily to give people the opportunity to hear the truth of the Word of God. And I believe God would have told us to launch the daily broadcast even if He knew no one would ever listen. That's how faithful He is! He is determined to give His witness.

We'll never know in this life all the people who have had a witness from God through the daily broadcast. It goes all over the world now. It's even in Eastern Europe and other places where people are hearing the Word for the first time in their lives.

One woman who lives in a remote city of the Ukraine was miraculously healed as she watched our broadcast. Earlier she had gotten saved while watching another Christian television program. She had never heard the gospel preached before she watched that broadcast. Her city is so isolated that at the time it didn't even have one church!

All of this woman's life, she had suffered from a huge growth on her back that kept her from walking straight. Then one day she saw our *Believer's Voice of Victory* broadcast. Later she testified to some Christian workers who visited her home, "As I watched Kenneth Copeland, he suddenly looked at me, pointed his finger and said, 'You're healed!' When he said that, I believed it—and the growth on my back burst and disappeared!" That woman heard the Word, acted on it in faith and received her miracle!

That's why you can't always judge the success of ministry outreaches by dollars and cents. God didn't say, "Go be a witness as long as it is a financial success." He just said, "Be a witness."

We're down to the last of the last days. God wants to do some mighty things to get His witness to all flesh—and I guarantee you, He will get them done! He will find someone who will be the witness He desires for any particular spot or individual on the face of the globe.

There has never been a more important hour than right now to live as part of the Church. God has a set time for the return of Jesus Christ, and He has determined, "Before that time, I will have My witness throughout the earth." You can count on that getting accomplished—and I want to help Him do it!

This is no time to hold back on what God is telling you to do. It may be the biggest assignment you have ever had. It may look impossible to you. But if God said to do it, put your foot in the water and do it! Be a part of God's witness to this generation!

WE CHOOSE OUR OWN OUTCOME

The secret to having things go well with us is to hear what God says about our lifestyle, our future and our destiny—and then to follow His counsel. That's what God was trying to get His people to give attention to in Jeremiah 11. He was giving them the same choice He gave Moses' generation all the way through Deuteronomy:

> **And say thou unto them, Thus saith the Lord God of Israel; Cursed be the man that obeyeth not the words of this covenant....**
>
> **Then the Lord said unto me, Proclaim all these words in the cities of Judah, and in the streets of Jerusalem, saying, *Hear ye the words of this covenant, and do them.***
>
> **For I earnestly protested unto your fathers in the day that I brought them up out of the land of Egypt, even unto this day, rising early and protesting, saying, Obey my voice.**
>
> **Yet they obeyed not, nor inclined their ear, but walked every one in the imagination of their evil heart: therefore I will bring upon them all the words of this covenant, which I commanded them to do; but they did them not.**
>
> **(Jeremiah 11:3, 6-8)**

Now, where have we read that kind of message before? Well, one place was in Deuteronomy 28. God speaks the end from the beginning, and He told Israel, "Hearken unto Me, and you will be blessed. Refuse to hearken, and these curses will come upon you" (vv. 1-2, 15, author's paraphrase).

Nothing has changed since God said that. Hear these words and do them. That's all any of us have to do to walk in God's blessings and avoid living under the curse of sin and death.

God did His very best to convince His people to turn back and follow Him. He gave them every opportunity to repent of their wicked ways, but they wouldn't listen to Him. Their hearts were hardened by their rebellion and unbelief.

So in Jeremiah 11:14, God reaches a verdict and tells the prophet Jeremiah:

> **Therefore pray not thou for this people, neither lift up a cry or prayer for them: for I will not hear them in the time that they cry unto me for their trouble.**

The Israelites of that day chose their own outcome. God had told them again and again, "This is the way it's going to be: You either go My way, which leads to victory and increase, or you go your own way to continual defeat and captivity." The people chose to go the way of rebellion, and their end was exactly what God had said it would be. They went into captivity.

We also choose our own outcome. Even though we are under a new and better covenant, we still have to choose to make Jesus the Lord of our lives in order to enter into that new covenant.

You may say, "Well, I just do my best in life. I'm a good person, but I don't believe in that 'being born again' stuff." The truth is that it doesn't matter *what* you believe about this subject—

the Bible is true anyway! Jesus said to Nicodemus, **"You *must* be born again"** (John 3:7, NIV). The only way to come into the covenant of peace with God is by making Jesus Christ the Lord of your life. It's your choice.

We have to choose to believe God's Word before He has the freedom to work in our lives and give us the good He has planned for us.

GOD IS YOUR SOLUTION, NOT YOUR PROBLEM

God chastises, or instructs, us with His Word. He doesn't cause our problems. He tells us, "If you do this, I'll bless you. If you don't do it, you open yourself up to the strategies of the enemy" (Deuteronomy 28:1-2, 15, author's paraphrase). So whose fault is it if we choose to do the wrong things and get into trouble? Ours. We made the choices.

When we get in a hard place, sometimes it's difficult for us to understand where the real problem lies. It's difficult for us to see that *we* are the ones who opened the door to our troubles. It's so much easier to think, *God has missed it here.* It's called deception.

It's also easy to look back at the Old Testament people and think, *Adam, how could you have been so foolish as to not obey God? Israel, why did you keep refusing to listen to the prophets God sent?*

But we can be just as foolish. We let ourselves get out of the will of God through disobedience, and then when things don't work for us and we struggle, we ask, "Lord, why did You let this happen to me? How come You're not doing something to get me out of this?"

I'll tell you something that will save you a lot of heartache: *It is never God's fault, and He is never your problem.* You have to get that truth down in your heart before the hard times come. Then the next time pressure hits and Satan tries to get you to blame

God, you can refuse to bow your knee. You won't budge, because you know beyond a shadow of doubt that *God is never wrong.*

You just say, "Lord, I don't understand what is going on here. But I know that You haven't missed it, because You are faithful. I believe I receive Your wisdom in this situation. Now I'm asking You, Lord, to show me what I need to do to establish victory."

Jeremiah didn't do that in Chapter 15. As he sat there feeling sorry for himself, he began to accuse God. (Surely none of us have ever done that, but Jeremiah did!)

Jeremiah had to endure all kinds of abuse from the Israelites whenever he went to prophesy to them. He was appreciated by hardly anyone except God.

Once the king secretly sent for Jeremiah at night and said, **"Is there any word from the Lord?"**

Jeremiah replied, **"There is...thou shalt be delivered into the hand of the king of Babylon"** (Jeremiah 37:17). That wasn't the word the king wanted, but that was the word from the Lord that Jeremiah had. What else could Jeremiah do but speak it forth even though the king put him back in prison?

Throughout his ministry, Jeremiah was treated badly by his countrymen. In Jeremiah 15:15, we see that he was feeling a little sorry for himself. He said, **"O Lord, thou knowest: remember me, and visit me, and revenge me of my persecutors; take me not away in thy longsuffering: know that for thy sake I have suffered rebuke."**

This was one of those "Lord, don't You care?" kind of days for Jeremiah. You know that kind of day—when everything is going wrong and you feel like praying, "Lord, don't You care about me? Don't You care what they are saying? Don't You care that this is happening?"

This was God's response to him:

> **Therefore thus saith the Lord, If thou return, then will I bring thee again, and thou shalt stand before me: and if thou take forth the precious from the vile, thou shalt be as my mouth: let them return unto thee; but return not thou unto them.**
>
> (Jeremiah 15:19)

Jeremiah had to return to the Lord. He had to get God's Word straight into his heart. He had to quit putting out vile unbelief, accusing God of not caring or not seeing. That's the same mistake you and I must be careful not to make.

If anyone has missed it, *we* have. God hasn't missed it. He's never wrong. He's never late. He is always righteous and just. We should walk in such reverence of Him that we dare not even consider that He might be slack in His work.

At times you may have thought, *I'm doing everything I can. I have even kept my confession right. I don't know why this isn't working for me. Why isn't God doing something for me?*

Then one day as you drive along in your car listening to a teaching tape, the Word you are listening to drops into your heart. Suddenly, God lets you see what a puny job you've actually been doing, and you just melt inside. You say, "Oh, God, forgive me. Lord, I repent. I see now what I've been doing wrong. Forgive me for that. I repent."

I know I'm not the only one who has lived through that scenario! But I thank God that I did. I don't want to get crosswise with God. I don't want to be self-righteous, thinking I'm right and God is missing it.

I'm sure God gets tired of hearing us say, "I've done every-thing I know to do!" It reminds me of my little grandson Max when he was learning how to sit still in kindergarten. Max and another little boy from church were having a hard time of it. They weren't accustomed to having to sit down for any length of time, so they had to be disciplined a lot for disturbing the class.

One day when Max got in trouble again, his mother sat him down to sternly talk to him about the problem.

Max immediately said, "Mom, I'm doing the best I can!"

"Max," his mother replied, "you're just going to have to do better."

"But, Mom," Max protested, "I told you I am doing the best I can!"

But, you know, Max wasn't doing the best he could. He found out after a little practice that he could do much better at sitting still in class.

You and I don't have the right to say, "I'm doing the best I can" to God, either. (Max ruined that excuse for me forever!) We have never yet done the best we could for God.

But you don't have to feel condemned about it. You are God's child; He expects to have to correct you at times. He doesn't hold that against you. Just be tenderhearted and quick to repent. Don't let anything get between you and God. Say, "God, I see where I missed it. I should not have doubted You. Please forgive me." Get cleansed by the blood of Jesus and start over!

IN THE POTTER'S HANDS

We should never lose sight of the fact that God corrects and instructs us for our good. Understanding that helps us to stay pliable in the Master's hands as He molds us into the image of Jesus.

Look at what God says in Jeremiah 18:6:

> **O house of Israel, cannot I do with you as this potter? saith the Lord. Behold, as the clay is in the potter's hand, so are ye in mine hand, O house of Israel.**

"Can I not do with you as the potter does with the clay?" You see, all God wants is to be free to work in our lives. He isn't trying to take something away from us. He is trying to *give* something wonderful to every one of us. That's why He tells us, "Hear Me. Do what I say. Follow My plan. Get in My Word. Listen to Me in your spirit. Let Me make you a vessel of honor."

Think back to the way you were when you were first born again, before the Word was ever planted in your heart. You were a sad story before the Potter began to mold and shape you, weren't you?

God has certainly done a wonderful work on my vessel of clay through the years. I mean, I was so timid when I was a new Christian that I couldn't get up in front of people. I didn't have much to say either. Those days are gone forever!

God develops authority and power in you as you walk in His Word. An inner confidence rises up because you know Who is inside you and Who you are following. You get the revelation of 1 John 4:4: **"Ye are of God, little children, and have overcome them: because greater is he that is in you, than he that is in the world."** Self-confidence can never compare to the confidence that the Word of God builds in your heart—an inner assurance so that you can face anything that comes your way because the Greater One lives in you. It's no longer self-confidence but God confidence.

As you honor God's Word, He will do more in your life than you could ever imagine. He will make you a vessel of honor, prepared unto every good work, fit for the Master's use. Second Timothy 2:19-21 says:

> **Nevertheless the foundation of God standeth sure, having this seal, The Lord knoweth them that are his. And, Let every one that nameth the name of Christ depart from iniquity. But in a great house there are not only vessels of gold and of silver, but also of wood and of earth; and some to honour, and some to dishonour. If a man therefore purge himself from these, he shall be a vessel unto honour, sanctified, and meet for the master's use, and prepared unto every good work.**

God will shape you into a vessel of love to help and encourage others. He will fashion you into a vessel of His power and of His Word so that the Word can come out of your mouth and set ·people free.

It doesn't even matter if your vessel has been damaged in some way in the past. Jeremiah 18:4 tells you how the Potter looks at a vessel that is marred: **"And the vessel that he made of clay was marred in the hand of the potter:** *so he made it again another vessel,* **as seemed good to the potter to make it."**

He can make you into another vessel. It doesn't matter what your situation is today or where you've come from. You may have been a prostitute or a thief or a murderer. God can make you a new vessel.

I know murderers on death row whom God has made into other vessels—beautiful, wonderful vessels. Vessels of love. Vessels of honor. The first time I visited the women on death row in a Texas prison, they got up and began to sing songs of praise. They ministered to me more than I ministered to them! They were so full of the joy of the Lord.

Now, I know that those women on death row are extreme cases. But I know people from every walk of life who have been transformed by the power of God. Some came out of terrible lifestyles in which they absolutely lived like dogs—but God made them into beautiful vessels. Today they are such tender-hearted people. They radiate the love of God.

God wants to work on *your* vessel, too. But it's up to you to let Him. Make the decision to place yourself completely in the Potter's hands. Let Him make you into the vessel of honor He desires you to be.

WHEN YOU FEEL LIKE QUITTING

We've seen one instance where Jeremiah felt sorry for himself and was tempted to blame God for his troubles. Let's look at a time when Jeremiah felt like quitting. Listen to his heart and how real he was in his communication with God:

> O Lord, thou hast deceived me, and I was deceived: thou art stronger than I, and hast prevailed: I am in derision daily, every one mocketh me. For since I spake, I cried out, I cried violence and spoil; because the word of the Lord was made a reproach unto me, and a derision, daily. Then I said, I will not make mention of him, nor speak any more in his name.
>
> (Jeremiah 20:7-9)

You know, I understand Jeremiah. He had one of those days which we can all relate to, when he thought, *I don't want to do this anymore! I'm tired of people treating me as if I were dirt. I'm tired of being a reproach. I'm tired of my family being ashamed of me. I'm tired of this dungeon.*

You have to remember, these men and women of God we read about in the Bible were human beings who lived in flesh-and-blood bodies. The Spirit of God was upon them, but they dealt with the same "I want to quit" emotions that many of us do at times. They had to walk by faith just like we do, and it wasn't easy.

It certainly wasn't easy for Jeremiah. In order to "keep on keeping on," he had to overcome enormous opposition that constantly arose because of his prophetic calling. But Jeremiah finally came to the realization that he couldn't give up. When he tried to quit, something would happen to him. He described it like this, **"In my mind and heart it is as if there were a burning fire shut up in my bones. And I am weary of enduring and holding it in; I cannot [contain it any longer]"** (v. 9, AMP).

Jeremiah had said to himself, *I'm just not going to do this anymore. I'm resigning from my prophet post!* But there was a fire shut up in his bones. He knew that he could not keep from speaking forth the Word of God. Holy Ghost fire was shut up in his bones and there was no stopping the call of God.

When you feel like backing out of God's call on your life, you just have to do the same thing Jeremiah did: Keep doing and saying and acting on what you know to do. God will always bring you out in victory. When you obey God, the rewards are tremendous.

One day the same people who once reproached you will come to you and say, "I need help. I'm going bankrupt!" or "I have cancer in my body. Please help me!" And if you stood strong in a time of trouble and pressure, you will be able to do just that!

SHEPHERDS AFTER GOD'S OWN HEART

People are always looking for leaders who can help them walk in victory and success. In the Church, God has set pastors, shepherds over His people to lead them into obedience by word and by example.

A good pastor makes all the difference. Jeremiah 23:4 gives us a picture of what God expects of a pastor: **"And I will set up shepherds over them which shall feed them: and they shall fear no more, nor be dismayed, neither shall they be lacking, saith the Lord."** God wants His shepherds to feed the people His Word so they don't live in fear or lack or dismay.

Looking back throughout the history of Israel, you will find that the people did much better at obeying God when they had a strong, godly leader. Every time the Israelites under Moses obeyed him, they experienced victory over their enemies. When they refused to obey at the border of the Promised Land, they suffered defeat. Years later, the younger generation was faithful to obey Joshua, and they went on to victory as they possessed the Promised Land.

A church that is led by a good pastor has a head start in learning to live in victory—if the pastor will first feed himself. The only way a pastor can feed the people and keep them free from lack and fear is to speak anointed words of life out of his spirit. So in order to speak *out of* his heart, he has to put God's Word *into* his heart!

A good pastor is a wonderful blessing to the Body of Christ. It's a mighty calling to be placed in leadership over a part of God's flock—especially when you consider how much God cares for each one of His children. God calls faithful shepherds and anoints them to feed His sheep and to teach them how to walk in His ways and stop the evil one from coming in and destroying their lives.

GOD'S WILL: THE HIGHEST AND BEST

Whatever God has called you to do, it's so important that you choose to follow His plan. Your entire future depends on how you hear and obey God. Not only your future on this earth, but also your future in eternity depends on what you do right now.

Jeremiah 29:11-14a in *The Living Bible* says:

> **For I know the plans I have for you, says the Lord. They are plans for good and not for evil, to give you a future and a hope. In those days when you pray, I will listen. You will find me when you seek me, if you look for me in earnest. Yes, says the Lord, I will be found by you.**

Find out God's plan for your life and dedicate to fulfilling His will for you. God says if you will seek Him, you will find Him.

Prayer of Consecration

Father, I offer myself as a vessel for You. I give You full freedom to work Your plan for my life. Mold me, lead me, direct me. I set myself to seek Your face, Lord, to discover the plan You have laid out for me. I want to fulfill all that You have planned for me!

THINK ON THESE THINGS

If God said to do it, put your foot in the water and do it!
Be a part of God's witness to this generation!

The secret to having things go well with us is to hear
what God says about our lifestyle, our future and
our destiny—and then to follow His counsel.

I'll tell you something that will save you a lot of heartache:
It is never God's fault, and He is never your problem.

As you honor God's Word, He will do more in your life than
you could ever imagine. He will make you a vessel of honor.

CHAPTER 9

SOW
OBEDIENCE...
REAP INCREASE

The more I study the book of Jeremiah, the more I desire in my heart to hear and do. The book is just full of that message because it's the answer to every situation.

You see, the entire kingdom of God operates by the law of sowing and reaping. It works *for* you or it works *against* you. If you sow obedience, you reap increase. If you sow rebellion, you reap defeat and bondage.

STAY FAITHFUL WHERE GOD PLANTS YOU

So throughout Jeremiah's ministry, "Hear and obey" was the message God gave him to speak. In Jeremiah 25:3, Jeremiah says this to the people of Judah:

From the thirteenth year of Josiah the son of Amon king of Judah, even unto this day, that is the three and twentieth year, the word of the Lord hath come unto me, and I have spoken unto you, rising early and speaking; but ye have not hearkened.

Imagine that—for 23 years Jeremiah kept telling the same people the same thing: "Nebuchadnezzar, the king of Babylon, is

coming to take you into captivity if you don't amend your ways." But for 23 years, those same people refused to listen!

Over and over in Scripture God says of His people, "They hear, but they don't comprehend. They see, but they don't really see." He also says that their hearts were "waxed gross," which means their hearts had become fat and dull. The people were spiritually dull of hearing (Isaiah 6:9-10; Matthew 13:13-15).

If things don't work out in a situation within a week or a month, we get discouraged. But Jeremiah had to stay in the same place and give the same message to the same unbelieving, disobedient people for more than 23 years! He continued after this until he spoke God's Word to a stiff-necked people who absolutely refused to hear for 40 years.

Think about it. What if you were called to a flock of people, and after 40 years of giving them the Word of God, they still wouldn't hearken to what you were preaching?

We can learn something from Jeremiah. In the natural, it would be easy to think in a situation like that, *I'm missing it. I must be in the wrong place. God has forsaken me. I've lost the anointing.* But Jeremiah stayed faithful to what God wanted him to do.

We, too, must stay faithful where God puts us. We have to stay close enough to God to know what He wants us to do—and then, like Jeremiah, we have to do it at any cost.

During Jeremiah's long ministry to the people of Judah, the devil probably whispered in Jeremiah's ear, *You're wasting your time, Jeremiah. These people aren't worth it. You have been in this place for 23 years, and you don't have one accomplishment to show for it! You haven't done one thing that has made any difference. You shouldn't even be a prophet if no one will listen to you!*

That is the kind of talk we must refuse to listen to, whether it comes from the devil, other people or our own minds. Once we find out what God wants us to do, we must be faithful to follow His instructions until He says, "OK, that's enough. Go do something else."

NEVER DEVIATE FROM THE CALL OF GOD

I love to read about Jeremiah. He was so bold, so courageous. He gave God his all.

Listen to what the people of Judah told Jeremiah after he gave them the word of the Lord:

> Now it came to pass, when Jeremiah had made an
> end of speaking all that the Lord had commanded him
> to speak unto all the people, that the priests and the
> prophets and all the people took him, saying, Thou
> shalt surely die. Why hast thou prophesied in the name
> of the Lord, saying, This house shall be like Shiloh,
> and this city shall be desolate without an inhabitant?
> And all the people were gathered against Jeremiah in
> the house of the Lord.
>
> (Jeremiah 26:8-9)

Jeremiah was telling the people the truth, but they didn't want to hear it. They wanted to kill the messenger for bringing the message of God.

But here's how Jeremiah responded to the people's threats:

> Then spake Jeremiah unto all the princes and to all
> the people, saying, The Lord sent me to prophesy against
> this house and against this city all the words that ye

153

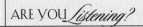
have heard. Therefore now amend your ways and your
doings, and obey the voice of the Lord your God.

(Jeremiah 26:12-13)

Jeremiah wouldn't compromise or back down from speaking
the message God had given him for the people. He was faithful,
and he was definitely not weak!

There was another time when Jeremiah was shut up in prison
and couldn't go preach to the people. So he "reprophesied"
everything to his faithful helper, Baruch, and instructed him to
write it down, word for word. Then Jeremiah told Baruch:

Therefore go thou, and read in the roll, which thou
hast written from my mouth, the words of the Lord in
the ears of the people in the Lord's house upon the
fasting day: and also thou shalt read them in the ears
of all Judah that come out of their cities.

(Jeremiah 36:6)

Baruch followed Jeremiah's instructions, reading Jeremiah's
words in the hearing of the people and princes of the kingdom.
The princes took Jeremiah's writings to the king. But as soon as
the document was read in the king's presence, the king's aide
took the parchment leaves and burned them in the fire (v. 23)!

What did Jeremiah do? He told Baruch, "Write my words
down again" (v. 28). Jeremiah was so loyal to God that he just
would not be shut up. He would not deviate from the call of
God. He would not fail to do what God had told him to do.

Jeremiah was faithful at any cost. He was put in a pit. He was
put in a dungeon. His life was continually threatened, but he
would not be stopped.

Jeremiah's testimony of bold obedience should inspire us to be just that faithful with what God has given us to do!

WHEN GOD'S MERCY OVERTAKES HIS JUDGMENT

God told the people of Judah to do very little in order to avoid going into captivity. They simply had to hear God and to give Him first place. They had to stop baking cakes for the "queen of heaven" and going after other gods (Jeremiah 7:18). If they would do these things, they would be saved from captivity and would remain in their land.

That doesn't seem like a lot to ask. Yet, the people wouldn't obey God. They gathered their wives and families together, shook their fingers in God's face and said, "We will not hearken. We're going to walk after our own desires and keep offering sacrifices to the queen of heaven. As long as we were doing that, things went well with us" (Jeremiah 44:15-17, author's paraphrase).

But it wasn't the queen of heaven who made things go well with them. God was having mercy on them for a space of time.

Isn't it amazing how foolish people can be? The people of Judah had only two choices: hear and do what God said, or go into bondage. And they chose bondage!

So the Lord told Jeremiah:

> **Stand in the court of the Lord's house, and speak unto all the cities of Judah, which come to worship in the Lord's house, all the words that I command thee to speak unto them; diminish not a word: If so be they will hearken, and turn every man from his evil way,**

> **that I may repent me of the evil, which I purpose to do**
> **unto them because of the evil of their doings.**
>
> **(Jeremiah 26:2-3)**

This scripture helped me see more clearly what the Bible means when it says that God repented. In Exodus 32:9-14, God was planning to wipe out Israel because of their disobedience. But when Moses stood in the gap and pleaded his case for the people, the Bible says that **"the Lord repented of the evil which he thought to do unto his people"** (v. 14).

That doesn't mean God suddenly decided He was wrong to bring judgment upon the people for their rebellion. He was absolutely right. When the Bible says that *God repented,* it means that His mercy overtook His judgment, causing Him to change direction for the nation of Israel.

God's people didn't deserve His mercy at all. We see a good example of this in Lamentations 3:22-23: **"It is of the Lord's mercies that we are not consumed, because his compassions fail not. They are new every morning: great is thy faithfulness."** God just can't help Himself. He is so good and His mercy is the result. He would not give up in His efforts to reach His people. He kept giving them one more opportunity, even though He knew they wouldn't repent and turn back to Him. He always had their welfare at heart, but eventually He couldn't keep an unrepentant, disobedient nation from going into captivity. Unless they changed, judgment was inevitable—not because God wanted it that way, but because they refused to hear Him.

You see, God isn't like the devil. He doesn't force His way into your heart. If you don't want Him, you won't have Him. He won't bother you. If you don't choose Him, He will allow you to choose your own destruction. God is up front with you. He speaks only truth.

The devil is a different story. He is a deceiver and a liar. He *will* try to force his way on you. He will try to trick you and tempt you into giving him your will.

But God won't do that. He is not a dictator or an outlaw like Satan is. God won't force your will; He waits for you to give it to Him. You have to choose to obey Him if you want God to manifest Himself in your life.

GOD WILL HAVE HIS WAY!

God couldn't prevent the people of Judah from suffering the consequences of their own disobedience, but in His mercy He did give them a ray of hope. Again and again, He warned them that if they persisted in walking in their own ways, a time was coming when they would be scattered among the nations (Jeremiah 9:16, 13:24). Then His mercy would say, "But I will gather you again" (Jeremiah 23:3, 29:14).

You see, God *will* have His way. That's why I'm going to stick with Him! There is no way the devil can win his bid for dominion. He has already been defeated by Jesus' death and resurrection, and he cannot overcome that defeat. It may look as if the devil is in control and his people are running things. But the Bible says God laughs at the wicked (Psalm 2:4)! He sees their day coming. He knows what will happen to them.

I'm telling you, no man or devil can get away from the law of sowing and reaping! I don't care how smart a person thinks he is or how much money he has, he won't be able to stop that law from operating(any more than he could stop the law of gravity. Seeds of obedience reap blessings just as seeds of rebellion reap calamity. It's a law of the kingdom, and it always comes to pass.

CALLED TO INCREASE

God also gave His people hope that increase and blessings would come to them, even in the midst of their captivity. That's just how merciful He is!

> **Thus saith the Lord of hosts, the God of Israel, unto all that are carried away captives, whom I have caused to be carried away from Jerusalem unto Babylon; Build ye houses, and dwell in them; and plant gardens, and eat the fruit of them; Take ye wives, and beget sons and daughters; and take wives for your sons, and give your daughters to husbands, that they may bear sons and daughters; that ye may be increased there, and not diminished.**
>
> **(Jeremiah 29:4-6)**

The people had turned their backs on God. They had essentially spit in His face, year after year after year. But God still wanted them to increase.

Throughout the Bible, it is obvious that God's people are called to increase. God's only intention for the Israelites under Moses and the people of Judah in Jeremiah's day was to do them good. He told them certain things to do so that they could have freedom and peace and live in victory. As verse 11 said, His plans for them were always plans for good, to give them a future and a hope.

It doesn't matter who you are—God has a good plan for you. You have a future with God. He's so good and so merciful. You are born of Him and that's the way He sees you. "That's My son!" "That's My daughter!"

Even natural parents have good plans for their children's futures. Of course, sometimes children don't walk in the good that their parents desire for their lives. But parents don't ever plan for tragedy, calamity, poverty, sickness and disease for their children. They plan for good.

Well, how much more does our Heavenly Father want a future and a hope for us?

Look at what He tells His people in Jeremiah 29:12-14:

> **Then shall ye call upon me, and ye shall go and pray unto me, and I will hearken unto you. And ye shall seek me, and find me, when ye shall search for me with all your heart. And I will be found of you, saith the Lord: and I will turn away your captivity, and I will gather you from all the nations, and from all the places whither I have driven you, saith the Lord; and I will bring you again into the place whence I caused you to be carried away captive.**

All the people had to do was seek God with all their hearts. Then they would find Him, and He would turn away their captivity.

That's what Daniel did. Seventy years later, while living as a captive in Babylon, Daniel found Jeremiah's writings about this, and Daniel began to seek the Lord.

The Bible says that Daniel had an excellent spirit and that no error was found in him (Daniel 6:3-4). He was a man of prayer. He was faithful. He wouldn't compromise, even if it cost his life. He served God continually.

What was Daniel's outcome? He received divine health. He was not harmed, even when thrown in a den of hungry lions. Instead, his enemies were destroyed. The Bible says he lived during the regimes of four kings—Nebuchadnezzar, Belshazzar,

Darius and Cyrus—and he prospered during every reign (Daniel 2:46-48, 5:29, 6:28).

Daniel totally fulfilled Jeremiah 29:11-15. When he sought God with all his heart, God heard his prayers, turning the captivity of His people and bringing them back to the land He had given them. Meanwhile, Daniel lived out God's good plan for his own life—a life of prosperity and peace, hope and blessing.

You see, God doesn't change. His Word doesn't change. You can count on God. He won't get up tomorrow and be different than He was today.

Why? Because God is right! He started out right, so He can't change anything about Himself. If He ever changed, He'd be wrong! That's why we can have a life of stability and peace when we walk with Him.

GREAT IN COUNSEL, MIGHTY IN WORK

Jeremiah 32:19 gives us two other characteristics of God's nature. It says He is **"great in counsel, and mighty in work."** These two characteristics go together. We take His counsel, and He does His mighty work!

God counsels us. He tells us what to do. But we have to *take* His counsel and act on it before it will do us any good.

Verse 19 goes on to say, **"For thine eyes are open upon all the ways of the sons of men: to give every one according to his ways, and according to the fruit of his doings."** Once again, this is the law of sowing and reaping in action. God gives to everyone according to his ways and according to the fruit of his doings.

The people of Judah reaped a harvest of sorrow according to the fruit of their doings. God said, **"They have turned unto me the back, and not the face: though I taught them"** (Jeremiah 32:33). It wasn't His fault they went into captivity, because He was great in counsel. They simply would not hearken to His instruction. Instead of lifting up holy hands before the Lord and worshiping Him, they turned their backs to Him.

That's something you don't want to do. Whatever God calls you to do, do it; don't turn your back on Him. If you do, you're in trouble because you have just hindered Him from working His good plan in your life.

Keep your face turned toward God all the time, ready to hear Him, ready to obey Him. Take His counsel. Answer the call. And once you have sown seeds of obedience, watch Him do a mighty work in your life. Remember, you are called to increase!

Prayer of Consecration

Lord, I set myself to seek Your face, to meditate on Your Word, to obey Your voice and to honor You in my words and in my actions all the days of my life.

You are great in counsel, Lord, and mighty in work! You are the great God! There is nothing too hard for You. Thank You for rising up in me by Your Spirit to counsel me. Thank You for being mighty in my life!

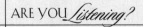

THINK ON THESE THINGS

The entire kingdom of God operates by the law of sowing and reaping. It works for you or it works against you.

God won't force your will; He waits for you to give it to Him. You have to choose to obey Him if you want God to manifest Himself in your life.

It doesn't matter who you are—God has a good plan for you.

You can count on God. He won't get up tomorrow and be different than He was today.

CHAPTER 10

OBEDIENCE FROM THE HEART

I want you to see that from the very beginning, God has wanted His people to be blessed—to multiply, to rule and to dominate the earth. Why? Because the earth and the fullness thereof belong to God, not to the devil. The devil has only been occupying it. He has had Adam's lease for a while, but Adam's lease is expiring.

The devil is called **"the god of this world"** (2 Corinthians 4:4) because this world in their spiritual blindness has followed him. But the people of God have always been able to dominate the laws of the world's system whenever they have risen up and obeyed God. We can live in God's light in a dark world. We can live in God's provision when the world is in lack. We can live in health when the world is sick. We can live in victory when the world is defeated. We can live in freedom when the world is bound. In fact, walking in obedience to God is the key to living free from the world's system.

God continually looks for people who will honor His Word with obedience so that He can do them good. Second Chronicles 16:9 says, **"For the eyes of the Lord run to and fro throughout the whole earth, to show himself strong in the behalf of them whose heart is perfect toward him."**

The Hebrew word for *perfect* refers to something that is devoted, consecrated, dedicated, loyal, faithful. God treasures a faithful heart!

Only you can decide whether or not you will be one of those who obeys God from the heart. Personally, I've made my decision. I'm going to be one of those people. I won't deviate from my call. I won't fall back from the Word. I'm determined to honor God by obeying Him!

A PROPHECY FULFILLED

The people of Judah refused to obey God, despite all His efforts to get them in a position to be blessed. Yet, even when they brought disaster upon themselves through their rebellion, He still looked ahead to a time when He could bless them again.

> **Behold, I will gather them out of all countries, whither I have driven them in mine anger, and in my fury, and in great wrath; and I will bring them again unto this place, and I will cause them to dwell safely.**
>
> **(Jeremiah 32:37)**

The Scripture talks about God gathering the Jewish people, Abraham's natural seed, from all over the world, especially from the region that today includes the former communist bloc nations of Eastern Europe (Jeremiah 31:8). It was only a generation ago that we saw this scripture fulfilled. When Israel became a nation again in 1948, a mass ingathering of Jews began from all over the world to their tiny, new nation.

If you have ever thought, *Will God's Word really work?* just read the Bible and then look at recent events! God's Word reaches through hundreds and even thousands of years to fulfill His plans and purposes.

The people who have been gathered from the four corners of the earth are now dwelling in the land of Israel. They aren't dwelling safely yet, but that day will come. God is gathering the natural seed of Abraham once more to the land He has given them. And He promised in Jeremiah 32:38-41:

> **They shall be my people, and I will be their God: And I will give them one heart, and one way, that they may fear me for ever, for the good of them, and of their children after them: And I will make an everlasting covenant with them, that I will not turn away from them, to do them good; but I will put my fear in their hearts, that they shall not depart from me. Yea, I will rejoice over them to do them good, and I will plant them in this land assuredly with my whole heart and with my whole soul.**

God is such a good and merciful God! Even though His people turned their backs on Him, His plan for their good continues without weakening. Every word He has said on their behalf will be fulfilled.

HEIRS TO THE COVENANT PROMISES

In Jeremiah 33:3, 6, God continues to talk about blessing the people of Judah:

> **Call unto me, and I will answer thee, and show thee great and mighty things, which thou knowest not....**
>
> **Behold, I will bring it [Jerusalem] health and cure, and I will cure them, and will reveal unto them the abundance of peace and truth.**

Now, it's important to understand that everything God did for His people was possible because He made a covenant with their forefather, Abraham. And God is just as loyal to you and me as He was to them. He is the God Who keeps covenant (Deuteronomy 7:9; Nehemiah 1:5).

Remember, Galatians 3:14-16, 29 says that we are the seed of Abraham and heirs to that covenant. We have been born into this position by accepting Jesus Christ as Lord and Savior. Through Jesus' death, burial and resurrection, God offers salvation to the nations who were previously without hope and without God in the world. All are invited into a covenant relationship with the Father through Jesus.

We have been adopted into the new covenant through the blood of Jesus. Not only do we now have all the benefits of the old covenant, but we have a new covenant established on better promises.

The new covenant includes a new heart! And as God said to the natural seed of Abraham, "All you have to do is call on Me, and I'll answer you," He is surely saying those same reassuring words to us today.

We must never forget, however, that all those wonderful covenant promises are based on our decision to honor God by hearing and doing His Word.

THE CHILDREN OF JONADAB: AN EXAMPLE OF OBEDIENCE

The word of the Lord came to Jeremiah concerning a family who obeyed and honored their father. God gave Jeremiah some unusual instructions.

> Go unto the house of the Rechabites, and speak
> unto them, and bring them into the house of the Lord,
> into one of the chambers, and give them wine to drink.
>
> (Jeremiah 35:2)

So Jeremiah took pots full of wine and set them before the Rechabites and said, "Drink this wine" (v. 5). However, the Rechabites refused to do it. They told Jeremiah:

> We will drink no wine: for Jonadab the son of
> Rechab our father commanded us, saying, Ye shall
> drink no wine, neither ye, nor your sons for ever....
>
> Thus have we obeyed the voice of Jonadab the son
> of Rechab our father in all that he hath charged us, to
> drink no wine all our days, we, our wives, our sons,
> nor our daughters.
>
> (Jeremiah 35:6, 8)

Think about that. This was generations after Jonadab, these people's forefather, had died. Yet they were still honoring their father with their obedience! And their faithfulness didn't go unnoticed. God used the obedience of the children of Jonadab as an example to the people of Judah:

> Then came the word of the Lord unto Jeremiah,
> saying, Thus saith the Lord of hosts, the God of Israel;
> Go and tell the men of Judah and the inhabitants of
> Jerusalem, Will ye not receive instruction to hearken to
> my words? saith the Lord.
>
> The words of Jonadab the son of Rechab, that he
> commanded his sons not to drink wine, are performed;
> for unto this day they drink none, but obey their father's

commandment: notwithstanding I have spoken unto
you, rising early and speaking; but ye hearkened not
unto me. I have sent also unto you all my servants the
prophets, rising up early and sending them, saying,
Return ye now every man from his evil way, and amend
your doings, and go not after other gods to serve them,
and ye shall dwell in the land which I have given to
you and to your fathers: but ye have not inclined your
ear, nor hearkened unto me.

(Jeremiah 35:12-15)

You can really see the Father's heart in this scripture. God
was saying to the people of Judah, "It looks to Me as if you
could do what the children of Jonadab did. They hearkened to
their father. Whatever he told them to do, they did it. That's all
I'm asking of you."

Then Jeremiah spoke a word from the Lord to the Rechabites:

Thus saith the Lord of hosts, the God of Israel;
Because ye have obeyed the commandment of Jonadab
your father, and kept all his precepts, and done according unto all that he hath commanded you: Therefore
thus saith the Lord of hosts, the God of Israel; Jonadab
the son of Rechab shall not want a man to stand
before me for ever.

(Jeremiah 35:18-19)

God takes your obedience very seriously because that is the
only way He can truly take His place as your God. He was so
impressed with the way the children of Jonadab honored the
words of their father that He blessed them and their children
forever. That means that somewhere in the world today, the sons

of Jonadab are still around. I would like to think that they are still being obedient!

GOD IS HONORED THROUGH OBEDIENCE

God has always wanted a family that will honor Him with their obedience like Jonadab's family honored him. Then He can get in the midst of them and do them good. As we've already seen from Deuteronomy 28, obedience causes you to live in the place of increase and blessing. God blessed Jonadab's whole family because they proved out what He wanted Israel to do—to honor Him by being obedient.

It's obvious when you study Israel, that is what God wanted for them. But in Jeremiah 22:21 He says, **"I spake unto thee in thy prosperity; but thou saidst, I will not hear. This hath been thy manner from thy youth, that thou obeyedst not my voice."** You see, God had made Israel prosperous, but they refused to acknowledge that and became disobedient. They failed to honor Him, so things were about to change for the worse for them. But that was never God's desire for Israel—nor for us.

God wants honor because He wants to be free to move and do us so much good that the world around us trembles at it. He wants to say about us what He said about Jerusalem: **"It shall be to me a name of joy, a praise and an honour before all the nations of the earth, which shall hear all the good that I do unto them: and they shall fear and tremble for all the goodness and for all the prosperity that I procure unto it"** (Jeremiah 33:9). The people around us ought to see God blessing us so much that they think, *I can't believe those people. They are so blessed! What are they doing that they are so blessed?* It honors God when we are obedient and then others can see that we are blessed because of our obedience to Him.

You know, the only way you can walk in the fear of the Lord and honor Him is by doing what He says. If He speaks to you and you turn your back on Him, you have dishonored Him as God. But the more determined you are to find out what God is saying so you can obey Him, the more honor you show to Him.

In 1 Samuel 2:30, God said, **"Them that honour me I will honour, and they that despise me shall be lightly esteemed."** That word *despise* means "to take lightly." You see, in order to overcome the evil, lack, poverty and sickness that is in the world, you can't take God's words lightly. You have to honor Him with everything you have and do whatever He tells you to do. That is where great blessing lies.

God asks in Malachi 1:6: **"A son honoureth his father, and a servant his master: if then I be a father, where is mine honour?"** He is still asking the same question today: "Where is My honor?"

If you honor God, He will honor you. If you treat Him as God in your life, He will manifest Himself as God in your life.

Now, is that fair? I believe that is very fair. To the extent we honor God and His Word, we will enjoy the manifestation of God in our lives.

Do you want great manifestation? Then open the way for God to work in your life by giving Him great honor. Seek His face. Spend time in His Word. Find out what He is saying to you and do it. Be quick to make changes. Be pliable to the Spirit of God.

HEART OBEDIENCE

God desires a people who will love Him and do what He says from their hearts so that He can do them good. That's the only way He can manifest Himself to do any good on the earth.

Psalm 145 says that God is good and He is good to all. He desires to do good because HE IS GOOD! He made it plain from the beginning that He wants to bless (empower to prosper) His people. He wants to take care of His family. He wants to prosper them and give them the wealth of the world. He wants to make them immune to every disease. He wants them to be the head and not the tail—above only and not beneath (Deuteronomy 28), and obedience is the key!

I believe that in this hour, God finally has a great mass of people all over the world with hearts to obey Him. I'm not talking about people who are good at keeping a set of religious rules. I'm talking about those who obey God from the heart because they love Him. They obey God because He is God and because they desire to give Him the honor due His Name. They obey, whether it's easy or hard, whether it's something they want to do or not. They are willing to step out and obey just because He said it. They have faith in Him.

You see, God doesn't talk to our heads, our wills or our bodies; He talks to our hearts. First Samuel 16:7 teaches us that God looks on the heart. And in 2 Chronicles 16:9, we find that the eyes of the Lord go to and fro throughout the whole earth, looking for that one whose heart is perfect—loyal, faithful, dedicated—toward Him.

The truth is that if our hearts are not committed to obeying God, we won't be able to control our bodies. In the natural we may try to do right, but if our efforts don't come from our hearts, we will fail. We can't walk after the flesh and enjoy the blessing of God. Romans 8:2-4 teaches us that the law of the Spirit of life in Christ Jesus makes us free from the law of sin and death by enabling us to walk in righteousness. Righteousness is God's way

of doing things. Walking in the ways of God causes all other things to be added unto you (Matthew 6:33).

God has told Kenneth and me to do things we absolutely didn't want to do. For instance, I said earlier that I didn't want to preach. Preaching didn't come naturally for me. Even today I would rather listen than speak. But I stepped out in faith and began to preach, regardless of my feelings about it, because I had a heart to honor and obey God. Oh, how it has blessed and enriched my life. I'm so glad I obeyed.

I also didn't want to lay hands on the sick. But God's direction to minister to the sick was the strongest instruction of any kind I have ever received from Him before or since. So I had to say, "I'll do it, Lord." There was no way I could deny that it was God calling me to that ministry.

As it turns out, praying for the sick has been one of the greatest blessings of my life! Actually, God's will always turns out to be a blessing when we hear from Him and then act on His words. I can testify that after walking with God for more than 32 years, *everything* He has told me to do has been a blessing. When you obey, God adds to you. He never diminishes you.

CORNELIUS: A WILLING HEART

In the New Testament, Cornelius, the centurion, is a good example of someone with a willing heart to obey God. Of all the gentiles on whom the Holy Ghost might have fallen, Cornelius was chosen because he had such a willing heart.

The angel told Cornelius what to do, and Cornelius did it. He sent for Peter and gathered all of his family at his house to hear what Peter had to say (Acts 10:30-33).

Cornelius didn't gather his household together for a nice little service. He wanted them all to hear the Word of the Lord. And Cornelius didn't just intend to hear; he had a heart to do. With a willing heart like that to work with, God had an open door to move! **"While Peter yet spake these words, the Holy Ghost fell on all them which heard the word"** (Acts 10:44).

Cornelius' heart was so devoted that while Peter was still speaking, the Holy Ghost fell on *all* of them! (I love that word *all* in the Bible!) Those people didn't know anything about the Holy Ghost falling. They didn't know what to expect. But they had hearts turned to hear God, and that's all He needed to manifest Himself in their midst!

I believe the Holy Ghost will manifest Himself in our midst today as well, whenever we reverence God and His Word. He will rise up in our hearts and give us answers to situations with which we've struggled, or fall upon all who sit in a congregation as the Word is preached from the pulpit. However God chooses to manifest Himself, the fact remains that freedom comes when we hear and reverence the Word of God. Notice what the Holy Spirit says about Cornelius. He was a devout man who feared God with all his house. He was a giver. He always prayed. He fasted. He obeyed what the angel said. He and his family gathered to hear all things that God commanded. His desire was to HEAR AND DO!

God found an obedient heart and poured out His Spirit. Now we know why Cornelius and his house were the first gentiles to receive the Holy Spirit.

HEARTS THAT ARE QUICK TO RECEIVE

God will manifest Himself to anyone who has a heart that is quick to hearken to God's Word—even if that person lives in the deepest part of a remote jungle. If necessary, the Lord Jesus Himself will appear to get His message to him! For instance, I have heard accounts from all over the world in which Jesus appeared to people who were caught up in other religions. It doesn't matter where you are; God will find you when you have a heart toward Him.

The people in the former Soviet Union nations have some of the most willing hearts to receive God's Word that Kenneth and I have ever seen in our lives. They grab hold of the Word and grow so quickly! They believe the Word of God and begin to do it. They could teach the rest of us a thing or two.

The *Believer's Voice of Victory* broadcast is on television daily in more than 60 cities across Eastern Europe, and we have found that the people there are so quick to believe. When we tell them to do something according to the Word, they simply hear it and then do it in faith. Many of them hear the truth in one 30-minute broadcast, it turns their lives around, and they get born again or miraculously healed.

One of the greatest testimonies I ever received from that region of the world was from a Ukrainian woman who was healed of several serious ailments in her body as a result of watching the broadcast. During the broadcast, she received an important revelation while listening to the message: The devil was the one afflicting her body.

This woman's leg was the first thing for which she received healing. I told the audience to pray with me and receive their healing. Later she went into her bedroom, lay down on the bed and promptly rebuked the devil off her leg—and it was instantly healed!

In her excitement, the woman got up and started running through the flat. She said in the letter that her husband thought she was crazy!

This woman had just received one revelation. That's all she had. But, you know, the early Church didn't have much more revelation than she did. The early believers knew that Jesus is Lord, that sickness is of the devil and that they were to rebuke it. They acted on what little they had—and turned the world upside down!

This woman had several other physical problems, and she dealt with them one by one the same way she had done concerning her leg. It wasn't long before she was healed of every one of them. Then she turned her sights on her husband, who suffered from high blood pressure and who was not a believer.

Reasoning that the devil had to be the author of her husband's high blood pressure, she laid hands on him and said, "By the Name of Jesus, Satan, leave my husband. You don't have any right to bother him," and commanded the sickness to leave him.

Not only was the husband healed of high blood pressure, but the woman must have cast out every devil he had! In her letter to us, she wrote that her husband changed. She said, "He told me that he always was so, that I just didn't notice it. But I knew how my husband was before, like a tornado, everything about getting crushed, shattered and broken. Even the glass in the door is still broken, though it was a year ago." Then she said, "Satan left him. Now it's like honeymoon again. We live in love and without quarrels." What a good example of hearing and doing!

What happened with this woman? She heard truth and found out who her real enemy was. She found out that God wanted her healed and that the devil was trying to keep that from happening.

So she started rebuking every evil work of the devil she could find in her life. In the process, she was delivered from every one of her ailments! She also cast out the demons afflicting her husband, and he was totally transformed.

Through this woman's simple testimony of faith, we see once more what great things God will do when we believe in our hearts that what He says is true, and then act like it's true! No matter where we live or what our circumstances are, the Word of God will produce victorious results and change our lives from calamity to blessing.

The following is an excerpt of the letter from this woman in the Ukraine, in her own words. This woman is like the woman with the issue of blood in Mark 5. She inspires me! I so cherish this letter, I want you to have a copy of it:

"I was told that you are sending books except *Laws of Prosperity* and second book by Gloria Copeland. I don't remember the title. We have these books to read, but we have a long waiting list to get them. We ask you urgently, please, send us your books. Those two books I mentioned, they are wonderful, even miraculous. We've never read anything like that before.[1]

"Also when I was listening to Gloria and was repeating after her and then started to experience this all myself. You know, my dear friends, it is working for me. My leg was hurting badly. I was not able to straighten it fully. But later, after the preaching I went to the bedroom, lay on the bed and started to repeat what Gloria taught to repeat and—miracle—my leg got straightened and was not hurting any more. I jumped up, started to run around the

---

[1] See the back of this book for a complete listing of materials by Gloria Copeland which can help you learn how to receive your healing.

flat. My husband was suspiciously looking at me. He was thinking that I lost my mind. Later I had headache, toothache, bladder was hurting and I got healing from all these things.

"Then my husband had high blood pressure and I laid hands on him and told, "By the Name of Jesus, Satan, leave my husband. You don't have any right to bother him" and commanded the sickness to leave him. And you know, miracle happened. Satan left him. Now it's like honeymoon again. We live in love and without quarrels. My quick-tempered husband is changed. I don't recognize him. It is amazing. I asked him, "What's up with you? You are different." And he told me that he always was so, that I just didn't notice it. But I knew how my husband was before, like a tornado, everything around getting crushed, shattered and broken. Even the glass in the door is still broken, though it was a year ago. I kept silence, but inside of me, in my soul, I praise Jesus that He is able to do miracles and humble even those who are unbridled. Dear friends, I can do all things with the Name of Jesus."

Prayer of Consecration

Father God, I love You and thank You for the Word of God. I thank You for stirring up my heart to take courage, to be faithful and to fulfill what You have called me to do at any cost.

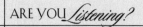

THINK ON THESE THINGS

God continually looks for people who will honor
His Word with obedience so that He can do
them good. God treasures a faithful heart.

The more determined you are to find out what God is saying
so you can obey Him, the more honor you show to Him.

If you honor God, He will honor you. If you treat Him as
God in your life, He will manifest Himself as God in your life.

Wrapped up in God's love...

CHAPTER 11

JESUS' EXAMPLE OF HEARING AND DOING

So far, we have talked about God's dealings with people in the Old Testament: first, Adam and Eve; then, the children of Israel under Moses and Joshua; and finally, the people of Judah during the time of Jeremiah. In each case, God's message was the same: "Hear Me and be diligent to do what I say. Then you can enjoy blessing and increase in every area of your life!"

That same divine message is taught throughout the New Testament as well. Look at the life of our supreme example, Jesus. He came to fulfill the will of God. He came to this earth as Jesus Christ the Righteous, without sin, born of a virgin. He was the Son of God in flesh, yet He still had to live every day hearing and doing God's Word in order to fulfill His destiny. If Jesus was required to hear and obey, I can guarantee that you will have to do the same if you want God moving supernaturally in your life.

You may be born again, a joint heir with Jesus, and you know heaven will be your home, but that doesn't free you from being obedient to God now. In fact, more than ever as a member of the family of God, you should be obedient.

Jesus set the example of obedience for His family, and He talked about it in Luke 8. Jesus' mother and brothers came to the place where He was teaching and asked to speak to Him, but they could not get near Him because of the crowd. Someone brought Him the message that His family was outside, but Jesus answered, **"My mother and my brethren are these which hear the word of God, and do it"** (v. 21). He wanted them to know that hearing and doing is the distinguishing factor of His family. He also lived out that example for us, so we have no excuse.

There is no doubt that Jesus walked circumspectly on this earth. We know from His own mouth that He always honored the Father and did the things that pleased Him (John 8:29, 49). Jesus had to walk this way because it is an unchangeable spiritual law: We must first hear and then do what God says. Good comes from God's hand as a result of our obedience.

DID JESUS PROSPER?

Throughout the Gospels, Jesus' words and lifestyle prove this law of God's kingdom. However, some people question whether or not Jesus lived in abundance while He walked on this earth. It's hard for them to believe that Jesus wasn't poor, although the Bible says He had a treasurer and that certain women ministered to Him out of their substance (John 12:6; Luke 8:3). Even as a young child, men brought Him gifts of gold, frankincense and myrrh—the Bible calls them "treasures" (Matthew 2:11). None of these scriptures indicate that Jesus was poor.

Here is something to think about. Jesus perfectly pleased God in His life. He did everything God told Him to do. So for Him not to increase would have been a failure of the Word of God. We would have to throw away half the Bible in order to make that possible!

God's written words have already been spoken out of His mouth. You can't change them. You can be blessed by them, but you can't change them. It is no more possible to walk with God in continual obedience to His Word and fail to increase than it is to jump off a building and fail to fall.

No, the Word is so clear there can't be any question about it. Since Jesus was wholly obedient, blessing and increase had to be the inevitable result.

OPERATING IN GOD'S KINGDOM

Now let's look at some scriptures to see how Jesus lived His life. As we study His life, remember this: If Jesus had to operate this way, we certainly must, as well, if we want to walk in victory.

Jesus came preaching, "The kingdom of God is here. You can get in on it, if you will. You can operate in it. You can be healed and set free. You can supernaturally enjoy the kingdom of God now" (Matthew 4:17; Luke 4:18-19, author's paraphrase). In Matthew 7:21, He taught people how to enter the kingdom of heaven:

Not every one that saith unto me, Lord, Lord, shall enter into the kingdom of heaven; but *he that doeth the will of my Father which is in heaven.*

The "king-dom" of heaven is where the *King* has *dominion.* He is sovereign, exercising supremacy in power and rank and authority. God's kingdom is a spiritual kingdom in heaven and over the earth. It is more powerful than the natural realm. When manifested in the earth, it takes authority over the natural realm.

You get in position for the dominion of heaven to break into this natural realm and change things by *doing the will of the Father in heaven.* In other words, when you do what God tells you to, His power and anointing begin to move in your behalf to help you overcome in every circumstance.

In John 8:23, Jesus talked about the kingdom of heaven and the kingdom of this world when He said, **"Ye are from beneath; I am from above: ye are of this world; I am not of this world."** The Pharisees lived under the world's system, while Jesus lived and operated in the kingdom of God, free from the world's system.

You can live and operate in the kingdom of God like Jesus did by doing what He did—by hearing from God and doing what He says. You may think it's hard to even hear from God, let alone do what He says. But John 10:27 says, **"My sheep hear my voice, and I know them, and they follow me."** In this scripture, the ability to hear and do is promised to those who belong to Jesus.

Also, if you're following the Good Shepherd, what you do will be good. Matthew 7:16-20 explains that good trees produce good fruit, and good fruit is the *evidence* that a tree is good: **"By their fruits ye shall know them"** (v. 20). I mentioned earlier that Jesus is called the True Vine in John 15:1. Verse 5 says, **"I am the vine, ye are the branches: He that abideth in me, and I in him, the same bringeth forth much fruit: for without me ye can do nothing."** Then verse 7 says, **"If ye abide in me, and my words abide in you, ye shall ask what ye will, and it shall be done unto you."** As we abide in Jesus and follow Him, the kingdom of God is established in our lives.

Now, understand that Jesus operated on earth as a man under the Abrahamic covenant, not as the Son of God. He came as a man in order to pay the price for man's sin. He was born of a woman, yet without sin because God was His Father (Luke 1:30-35). He had a body of flesh, a sinless spirit and the Spirit of the Lord upon Him.

Miracles took place in Jesus' ministry because God finally had a totally obedient man through Whom He could work.

Jesus said, **"I am the door"** (John 10:7-10). He was the open door for God to move and manifest the kingdom of heaven in this natural realm. The dead were raised, the maimed were made whole, the sick were healed, and the fish and loaves were multiplied because of Jesus' faith, His honor of God and His steadfast obedience.

Jesus was anointed by the Holy Ghost with power and given authority to fully represent His Father and His kingdom on this earth. Acts 10:34-38 says:

> **Then Peter opened his mouth, and said, Of a truth I perceive that God is no respecter of persons: But in every nation he that feareth him, and worketh right- eousness, is accepted with him.**
>
> **The word which God sent unto the children of Israel, preaching peace by Jesus Christ: (he is Lord of all:) That word, I say, ye know, which was published throughout all Judaea, and began from Galilee, after the baptism which John preached; How God anointed Jesus of Nazareth with the Holy Ghost and with power: who went about doing good, and healing all that were oppressed of the devil; for God was with him.**

As His Body, we are called and anointed by the same Spirit to do the same thing.

We will see greater and greater manifestations of these heavenly breakthroughs in our day. The more we follow Jesus' example—walking in God's Word, doing what He says, honoring Him and being diligent in our spiritual walk—the more we open the door for the glory of God to be manifested in our lives and in the lives of those to whom we minister.

FREEDOM FROM THIS WORLD'S SYSTEM

As we've already seen, Jesus operated independent from the world's system. The devil couldn't touch Him or bind Him up in any way until the day that He laid down His life of His own accord in obedience to God. He talked about this in John 10:15-18:

> I lay down my life for the sheep. And other sheep I have, which are not of this fold: them also I must bring, and they shall hear my voice; and there shall be one fold, and one shepherd. Therefore doth my Father love me, because I lay down my life, that I might take it again. No man taketh it from me, but I lay it down of myself. I have power to lay it down, and I have power to take it again. This commandment have I received of my Father.

Walking free and in obedience to God, everywhere Jesus went, He set other people free from the world's system of bondage and brought them into God's kingdom and God's way of doing things. But they had to hear His voice and obey it to come into the freedom of the Father's kingdom. In fact, in John 8:24 Jesus said, **"If ye believe not that I am he, ye shall die in your sins."**

Jesus told God's people how to escape the world's system of calamity and come into the blessing of the kingdom of God. It wasn't complicated. Anyone could do it if they chose. They had to hear Jesus' words and act on those words by believing in Him and receiving Him as the Son of God.

The Apostle Paul reveals the rest of the story: **"Giving thanks unto the Father, which hath made us meet to be partakers of the inheritance of the saints in light: Who hath delivered us from the power of darkness, and hath translated us into the** kingdom of his dear Son: In whom we have redemption through his blood, even the forgiveness of sins" (Colossians 1:12-14). We have already made the great escape! When we accepted Jesus Christ as Lord and Savior, we were translated out of the kingdom of the curse and into the kingdom of blessing!

HOW TO STAY IN FELLOWSHIP WITH THE FATHER

In John 5:30 (AMP), Jesus tells us how He conducted His personal life and reveals to us how to live in God's kingdom—under God's system.

> **I am able to do nothing from Myself [independently, of My own accord—but only as I am taught by God and as I get His orders]. Even as I hear, I judge [I decide as I am bidden to decide. As the voice comes to Me, so I give a decision], and My judgment is right (just, righteous), because I do not seek or consult My own will [I have no desire to do what is pleasing to Myself, My own aim, My own purpose] but only the will and pleasure of the Father Who sent Me.**

That's the way Jesus lived—hearing from God and obeying Him in everything.

This is a very important scripture to me. Back in the early days when I was just beginning to learn about these scriptural principles, the Lord opened this verse to me. At that time I was getting up every morning at 5:30 to have time with Him. So even the chapter and verse, 5:30, blessed me! I was seriously believing God to help Ken and me better know and understand His will for our lives.

Looking at how Jesus conducted His life provides a good example for all of us. Jesus lived and ministered successfully on this earth by hearing and doing what He heard from the Father. Jesus had no sin in Him, but He still had to do what it takes to stay in that place of obedience. When you think of it, Jesus lived the same way in earth as He had always lived in heaven. He had to spend time in the presence of His Father, praying and communicating with Him. He had to hear from God and get direction. His total dependence was on God and His way of doing things. He had to dominate His body and make it do the things that would please God.

The Scripture says that Jesus was tempted in all things just as we are (Hebrews 4:15). Yet He walked such a straight line before God that He never deviated, not one single time. He never failed to let God be God.

We have been born again to live the same way. God gave us new hearts and put His Spirit inside us so we can hear and do whatever He tells us to do. Everything in our lives should revolve around this one central thing.

Ezekiel 36:24-28 describes the change that has occurred in us, enabling us to hear and do:

> For I will take you from among the heathen, and gather you out of all countries, and will bring you into your own land. Then will I sprinkle clean water upon you, and ye shall be clean: from all your filthiness, and from all your idols, will I cleanse you.
>
> A new heart also will I give you, and a new spirit will I put within you: and I will take away the stony heart out of your flesh, and I will give you an heart of

flesh. And I will put my spirit within you, and cause you to walk in my statutes, and ye shall keep my judgments, and do them. And ye shall dwell in the land that I gave to your fathers; and ye shall be my people, and I will be your God.

If you are too busy to spend time with the Lord every day before you go out into the world and deal with situations and people, you are just too busy. You need to make some changes in your life, because the key to living a good life and a free life is taking the time to hear from God and doing what you hear.

I'm telling you, I wouldn't care a thing about living if I couldn't have God move in my life on a daily basis. I love living in total dependence on God because I trust Him. Those who live without God on this earth have no choice but to live in constant fear, unrest, turmoil and insecurity.

There is no security on the earth without God. But when you are in constant fellowship with Him, you can enjoy total peace and security in Him.

FREEDOM COMES IN DOING THE WILL OF GOD

In John 8:31-32, Jesus said those who believed on Him could walk free from the world's system just as He did:

If ye continue in my word, then are ye my disciples indeed; And ye shall know the truth, and the truth shall make you free.

What was Jesus talking about here? Hearing and doing the Word. He was saying, "If you will hear My Word and obey it, you will be free as I am free."

Freedom is found in doing the will of God. People in the world don't understand that principle. They think that obeying God results in bondage because they won't be able to do what their flesh wants to do.

But those people don't know what freedom really is. They are the ones who live in bondage. They know what it is to sin. They know how to do whatever makes them temporarily feel good. But they don't know the joy of the Lord or the freedom that stays with you and me every day of our lives as we listen to the Word and receive it as revelation into our hearts. They have never experienced the peace of God. God's peace is the peace that comes from being whole—nothing missing, nothing broken.

Jesus said that if we would continue in His Word, we would live free—free from oppression, free from lack, free from sickness and disease. And I'm telling you from personal experience, that is absolutely true.

But you have to continue. You can't give up and quit somewhere in the middle of this life of faith. You have to determine to continue and continue and continue! Keep doing what you know to do. The more you know of the Word—the more you receive God's words and let them live and abide in your heart—the freer you become.

Jesus pinpointed the problem with those who wouldn't receive Him: **"I know that ye are Abraham's seed; but ye seek to kill me, because my word hath no place in you"** (John 8:37).

Jesus had already told them, "You are operating down here on a lower plane. I'm from above; you are from beneath. You are of your father the devil, who was a liar from the beginning. You are in darkness, but I have the truth and the light of God" (John 8:23, 44-45, author's paraphrase).

These people wouldn't receive what Jesus said. In fact, Jesus said they could not hear His words. They were believing the words of the devil instead and obeying him. They believed the devil's lies instead of God's truth. Jesus said, **"He that is of God heareth God's words"** (vv. 43-47).

THE WISE MAN VS. THE FOOLISH MAN

Jesus continually taught on the importance of hearing and doing the Word. Let's look again at Jesus' message in Matthew 7 about life from above. Verses 24-27 say this:

> **Therefore whosoever heareth these sayings of mine, and doeth them, I will liken him unto a wise man, which built his house upon a rock: And the rain descended, and the floods came, and the winds blew, and beat upon that house; and it fell not: for it was founded upon a rock.**
>
> **And every one that heareth these sayings of mine, and doeth them not, shall be likened unto a foolish man, which built his house upon the sand: And the rain descended, and the floods came, and the winds blew, and beat upon that house; and it fell: and great was the fall of it.**

In this parable, Jesus is showing us the difference between a wise man and a foolish man(both in their actions and in their outcomes. A wise man hears and does what God says. He and his house will be left standing after the storms of life come.

A foolish man also hears, but that is as far as he goes. He doesn't act on God's words. So when a storm of adversity hits his life, his house has no foundation. He has nothing on which to stand. He did not follow through with doing what he heard. Jesus teaches us it is foolish to disobey God. When trouble comes, God has no opening into your life through which to bring deliverance. Disobedience says, "I'm choosing my way, not God's way." God allows you to choose!

Both men heard the same words—words that came from heaven to make men free of calamity. Both men experienced the storm. One was willing to live and operate in God's system. The foolish man refused and built his house on the sand. Great was the destruction of his house. He is the one who determined his future by what he did with the word he heard.

BORN TO OPERATE IN GOD'S SYSTEM

God has a system. He has a way of doing things that always works. As believers, we have been born again to operate in His system. Only His system produces life.

The Word of God works in nations where nothing else is working. There is little money and even less prosperity in these struggling nations. Yet we receive testimonies all the time from people whom God has blessed despite the desperate poverty that surrounds them. These people begin to honor God and tithe on their meager amount of money, and God begins to increase and prosper them.

One couple living in Eastern Europe wrote us that for more than two years they had been requesting a better place to live from government authorities. Then they started planting the Word in their hearts and making God's way their way. It wasn't long before God's system overpowered the world's way of doing things, causing the communist government to grant that couple's long-awaited request for a bigger flat. When God begins to change circumstances for His obedient people, not even governments are strong enough to stop His blessings. The Word of God brings freedom regardless of natural circumstances. Here is part of their letter:

Hello dear Kenneth, Gloria and the Kenneth Copeland Ministries!

Sorry for not answering to your letter at once, but we have our address changed because *we've got a new flat!!!*

If you still have my last letter where I was asking you for help and advice about how should we continue to live, it would not be difficult for you to compare how our life has changed with your help.

For more than two years we had had court sessions which always ended up in favor of those in power. We had a miserable life at place where we had no electricity, no water, no heating. And all that has changed so unexpectedly after I read the books by Gloria and Kenneth Copeland. [Kenneth and I know it's because of the Word of God in the books.]

We received Jesus as the Lord of our life; we began seeing things, events, people, etc. around us differently. I stopped asking the court or director of our plant— anybody, for improving our living conditions. All my requests were in my prayers to Jesus. And I could feel your support. Thanks!

Just before the end of the last year, instead of usual refusal, my husband unexpectedly got the warrant for a three-room apartment. As our town is a small one, everyone in town knew about our lawsuit with the local authorities. People were saying that we had no chance.

But you cannot imagine how they all were shocked, including even those among authorities and from the office of public prosecutor, when they learned that we won the case.

Even we ourselves were surprised about how and who could change the judges' minds. But later we understood—as we asked nobody but Jesus for help, so it was Him. Glory to Jesus! We are so grateful to our Lord for not leaving us in trouble.

Christians who live like the world are not walking in God's system. But things turn for good to those who obey God and do what He says. God's kingdom will manage the natural realm for a believer who keeps covenant with God.

Breakthrough takes place for those who operate according to the laws of the kingdom of heaven. From now until Jesus' return, this generation is going to enjoy more of the manifestation of God than ever before in the history of the Church. We will see more light, more increase, more blessings and more of God's power.

Take the time to diligently seek to find out what God says about how to live, then make His way your way. Jesus said in Matthew 6:33, **"Seek ye first the kingdom of God, and his righteousness; and all these things shall be added unto you."**

God is no respecter of persons. His Word will work for you the same way it worked for Jesus! The only way to walk in victory in this life is to dedicate to living in the kingdom of God. The way you do that is by seeking first the kingdom of God—His way of doing and being right. Then as you hear and obey God's Word, everything else will be added to you. His Word is your lifetime guarantee to victory!

Prayer of Consecration from Ephesians 1:17-19

Father, I pray that You, the God of our Lord Jesus Christ, the Father of glory, may give unto me the spirit of wisdom and revelation in the knowledge of Jesus Christ; that the eyes of my understanding may be enlightened so that I may know what is the hope of His calling, and what the riches of the glory of His inheritance is in the saints, and what is the exceeding greatness of His power toward me.

THINK ON THESE THINGS

Jesus perfectly pleased God in His life.
He did everything God told Him to do.

When you do what God tells you to, His power
and anointing begin to move in your behalf
to help you overcome in every circumstance.

Jesus lived and operated in the kingdom
of God, free from the world's system.

Jesus lived and ministered successfully on this earth
by hearing and doing what He heard from the Father.

Jesus lived the same way in earth
as He had always lived in heaven.

Freedom is found in doing the will of God.

CHAPTER 12

A vital revelation that Jesus shared on the subject of hearing and doing is found in Mark 4. This chapter is about the relationship between hearing and increase.

In the parable of the sower, Jesus teaches us how to be fruitful in God's kingdom and how to avoid being unfruitful. And guess what? It's totally dependent on how we hear and understand the Word.

And he taught them many things by parables, and said unto them in his doctrine, Hearken; Behold, there went out a sower to sow: And it came to pass, as he sowed, some fell by the way side, and the fowls of the air came and devoured it up.

And some fell on stony ground, where it had not much earth; and immediately it sprang up, because it had no depth of earth: But when the sun was up, it was scorched; and because it had no root, it withered away.

And some fell among thorns, and the thorns grew up, and choked it, and it yielded no fruit.

And other fell on good ground, and did yield fruit that sprang up and increased; and brought forth, some

thirty, and some sixty, and some an hundred. And he
said unto them, He that hath ears to hear, let him hear.

(Mark 4:2-9)

TRUE BIBLE HEARING

Before we study this parable, notice what Jesus said when He
finished relating it to the people: **"He that hath ears to hear, let
him hear"** (v. 9).

That word *hear* in this verse isn't just talking about hearing
with your physical ears. True Bible hearing includes not only
hearing what God says, but comprehending what He means,
receiving it in faith and meditating on it until it is planted in
your heart so that you do it.

You see, people can go to theological seminaries and study
the Word year after year, and still graduate with absolutely no
revelation knowledge whatsoever to take with them! That is *not*
the kind of hearing Jesus is referring to here in Mark 4.

When the knowledge of God's Word comes to a person's
heart, understanding (revelation) enables him to walk it, talk it
and apply it to his life. Living the Christian life is no longer a
matter of keeping a set of rules and regulations. Instead, it
becomes a supernatural walk of following God in the spirit,
unhindered and undefeated.

THE MYSTERIES OF THE KINGDOM

When he [Jesus] was alone, the Twelve and the others
around him asked him about the parables. He told
them, "The secret of the kingdom of God has been

given to you. But to those on the outside everything is said in parables."

(Mark 4:10-11, NIV)

Jesus began to give the disciples revelation understanding of the words He had spoken—knowledge hidden from those outside God's kingdom. *The Amplified Bible* says it this way:

> To you has been entrusted the mystery of the kingdom of God [that is, the secret counsels of God which are hidden from the ungodly]; but for those outside [of our circle] everything becomes a parable.
>
> (Mark 4:11)

You see, it has been granted unto us as God's covenant people to know and understand the hidden mysteries of God. Proverbs 2:7 says that God stores up His wisdom for the righteous.

People who are not in right-standing with God can't understand the wisdom of God or operate in it. It is hidden from them. They don't qualify, but we who are born into the kingdom have "top secret clearance"! God wants us to have understanding, so He lights our candles by His Spirit with the Word of God and reveals the secrets of His kingdom. Proverbs 20:27 says, **"The spirit of man is the candle of the Lord, searching all the inward parts of the belly."** And Mark 4:22 says nothing is hidden from us. The secrets of God's kingdom are waiting to be revealed to those who want them enough to spend time with the One Who knows all secrets.

Jesus asked the disciples, **"Do you not discern and understand this parable? How then is it possible for you to discern and understand all the parables?"** (Mark 4:13, AMP).

In other words, "If you don't learn this secret of the kingdom, how are you going to get anything?" Jesus was saying that the operation of the kingdom of God is revealed in this one parable! He emphasized its importance by saying, **"Give attention to this!"** (v. 3, AMP). It was necessary for the disciples to understand this parable.

Hidden in this parable is what Jesus called **"the mystery of the kingdom of God."** In this message Jesus teaches us how to get the kingdom of God manifested in this natural earth realm. Jesus' message that day is the revelation of how to receive the power of God to meet any need.

To have the hidden wisdom of God that meets every need, we must desire it enough to go after it with all our hearts. The Bible term is *seek*. In Matthew 6:33, God not only says "seek," but "Seek first the kingdom of God." That means to go after with strong, intense desire "in the sense of coveting earnestly, striving after"[1] knowledge of God's kingdom.

Another word God frequently uses to tell us how to be able to live after God's way of doing things is *diligence*. The dictionary definition of it is "perseverance";[2] "steady application in business of any kind; constant effort to accomplish what is undertaken."[3] An example would be Deuteronomy 28:1:

> **And it shall come to pass, if thou shalt hearken**
> **diligently unto the voice of the Lord thy God, to**
> **observe and to do all his commandments which I**

---

[1] W. E. Vine, *Vine's Expository Dictionary of Biblical Words* (Nashville: Thomas Nelson Publishers, 1985), p. 558.

[2] *Webster's New World Dictionary of American English,* 3rd college ed. (New York: Prentice Hall, 1994), p. 386.

[3] Noah Webster, *An American Dictionary of the English Language,* 1828, facsimile 1st ed. (San Francisco: the Foundation for American Christian Education, 1995), 1:61.

command thee this day, that the Lord thy God will set thee on high above all nations of the earth.

Diligence is a Bible key to walking with God. You will never be able to live in the supernatural power of God without enough desire to be diligent. However, the more time you spend with God, the greater your desire becomes. The more revelation you receive, the hungrier you get for more.

Matthew's account of this parable makes it clear: Those who hunger for more get more.

> **Then the disciples came to Him and said, Why do You speak to them in parables? And He replied to them, To you it has been given to know the secrets and mysteries of the kingdom of heaven, but to them it has not been given. For whoever has [spiritual knowledge], to him will more be given and he will be furnished richly so that he will have abundance.**
>
> **(Matthew 13:10-12, AMP)**

So, the person who has revelation knowledge—or understanding—of spiritual things, to him will be given more. "Get this," Jesus said. Increase is in hearing with understanding. This entire teaching depends on hearing the Word of God and understanding it.

Jesus went on to say, **"But from him who has not, even what he has will be taken away"** (v. 12, AMP). He was talking about those who have no understanding of spiritual things.

We have already seen that, in Israel's history with God, the people deliberately shut their ears to the things God told them. They said, "We don't want to follow You, God. We are not going to hearken. We are going to do things our way." God called it walking in the imaginations of their own evil hearts (Jeremiah 7:24).

The ones to whom Jesus spoke this message were the same as in Jeremiah's day. Jesus couldn't reveal the mysteries of the kingdom to them. Instead, He talked to them in parables, **"because having the power of seeing, they do not see; and having the power of hearing, they do not hear, nor do they grasp and understand"** (Matthew 13:13, AMP). Israel's heart had grown dull through disobedience, so they couldn't receive God's mysteries. They were not honoring God and His Word in their lives but were caught up in the tradition of men.

But to the disciples Jesus said, **"Blessed are your eyes, for they see: and your ears, for they hear"** (Matthew 13:16). That's where blessing lies—in hearing and receiving revelation of God and His kingdom.

Only to those who receive Jesus as Savior and Lord—those who are born of God—can the hidden mysteries of God's kingdom be revealed. Wherever they are, if they will seek God with their whole heart, the kingdom of heaven will be manifested.

WITNESSES TO THE KINGDOM

The King dwells within us through the Holy Spirit. His dominion is inside us. The authority in His Name has been given to us. He is the Victor in three worlds: in heaven, in earth and under the earth. He has the keys to hell and death, and He said to us, "Go in My Name and cast out devils. Preach the good news, and those who believe will be saved, healed and set free" (Mark 16:15-18).

We are to be witnesses to the manifested kingdom of God—not only with our mouths, but with our lives. It isn't a good testimony to the power of God when we can't pay our bills or when our church has to meet in an old, run-down building because we are living defeated lives.

Look at Israel, for example. God wanted the world to fear and respect them. He wanted the world to see that He was with His people, working on their behalf. He wanted them to know that there was a God in Israel named Jehovah!

That's what happened with Rahab and the people of Jericho. When the two Israelite spies came to gather information about Jericho, Rahab told them that they had heard about the parting of the Red Sea and the other miracles that God performed to bring them out of Egypt. She said, **"As soon as we had heard these things, our hearts did melt, neither did there remain any more courage in any man, because of you: for the Lord your God, he is God in heaven above and in earth beneath"** (Joshua 2:11).

That's the kind of testimony the Church should have today. People should look at the Body of Christ and say, "Those are the people whom God has blessed! I want to join them. They have victory." They will want to accept Jesus as Lord and Savior.

For instance, at our recent meeting in Riga, Latvia, a 17-year-old boy was miraculously healed. This boy's twisted legs had prevented him from walking all his life. But that night he walked onto the platform and danced and shouted and praised God for his healing.

Well, people saw that young man when he went back home. They saw someone who was born with twisted, crippled legs and is now walking!

That's the kingdom of God in manifestation! That's also the kind of witnesses we are to be, allowing God to manifest His love and power through us wherever we go. The Lord our God, He is God in heaven above and in earth beneath!

FOUR CATEGORIES OF PEOPLE

When Jesus explained the parable of the sower to His disciples, He said, "The sower sows the Word," and then described four different types of ground in which the seed—the Word of God—was sown: the ground by the wayside, the stony ground, the thorny ground and the good ground. These four types of ground represent the hearts of four different categories of people.

All four categories of people heard the Word of God, but what they did with what they heard determined their futures. Some of them refused to receive the Word at all, so they didn't receive any benefit. Some had no root, and they let the devil talk them out of what they had heard. Some received the Word, only to allow the things of this life to have first place in their hearts and overcome it.

Of the four types of hearers of the Word, only one produced fruit—the one who heard and then obeyed what he heard.

We are going to learn more about these four categories of ground. That way we can make sure we fit in the "good ground" category that yielded a harvest!

There was never any problem with the seed (Word) in any example—only the ground (heart). Andrew Murray says that the Word of God is like a natural seed: everything depends on the treatment it receives.

THE GROUND BY THE WAYSIDE

Let's *hear* what Jesus says as He begins to explain this parable to His disciples:

Now the parable is this: The seed is the word of God. Those by the way side are they that hear; then

cometh the devil, and taketh away the word out of their hearts, lest they should believe and be saved.

(Luke 8:11-12)

The first group of people is the ground by the wayside. Before these people ever believe, the devil comes and steals God's Word. These do not even believe God's Word enough to be saved. Before the seed can get into the ground, it is devoured. They are like the people in Jeremiah's day when they gathered with their wives and said to the prophet, "We will not hear you, but we will do whatever comes out of our own mouth. We will bake cakes to the queen of heaven" (Jeremiah 44:16-19).

This group has no understanding or revelation of what they hear. It is easy for the devil to take away the seed.

All through Mark 4, it is clear that we have to receive revelation, understanding and insight about what we hear in order for it to do us any good. We can't live by God's Word unless we understand it and know how to apply it to our own lives. That's why God sent us His Spirit to teach us and lead us into all truth—to keep us from being "wayside" hearers.

Jesus encountered a lot of "wayside" hearers during His earthly ministry. He was a superb teacher, but that didn't mean everyone would believe what He said. Many of those who heard Jesus preach the Word would *not* believe. This was especially true of those who were trained in religious tradition and unbelief like the scribes and Pharisees. They wanted to dispute Jesus' words instead of receive them. It is still that way today.

Jesus' answer to the scribes and Pharisees was:

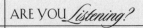

> **Why do ye also transgress the commandment of**
> **God by your tradition?... Thus have ye made the**
> **commandment of God of none effect by your tradition.**
>
> **Ye hypocrites, well did Esaias prophesy of you,**
> **saying, This people draweth nigh unto me with their**
> **mouth, and honoureth me with their lips; but their**
> **heart is far from me. But in vain they do worship me,**
> **teaching for doctrines the commandments of men.**
>
> **(Matthew 15:3, 6-9)**

When we hear the Word on any given matter, we all have a choice whether to receive it or reject it. Every time we reject one of God's promises, we disqualify ourselves from receiving that particular blessing.

For instance, someone might hear a sermon on prosperity and think, *I've been taught all my life that God is in favor of poverty. Now I'm hearing that He wants me to have abundance! That's just too good to be true.*

By leaning on the tradition of man that has been taught, that person is disqualifying himself from receiving the abundance God wants to give him. He is allowing his past training to refuse the Word of God so that it bears no fruit in his life. Remember Jesus said, **"Their eyes *they* have closed"** (Matthew 13:15). It is man's choice to reject or believe what God says. But those who refuse His words will have no understanding and no harvest. Before the seed ever got below the surface of the ground by the wayside, the birds came and devoured it. That left nothing in the ground to bring forth harvest. Seed has to get in the ground and stay there. Word has to get in the heart and abide there (John 15:7).

THE STONY GROUND

Now let's look at the second type of ground that Jesus described: This group does a little better but still has no harvest.

> **And these are they likewise which are sown on stony ground; who, when they have heard the word, immediately receive it with gladness; And have no root in themselves, and so endure but for a time: afterward, when affliction or persecution ariseth for the word's sake, immediately they are offended.**
>
> **(Mark 4:16-17)**

When this group heard the Word, they received it. They believed it. They let its truth into their heart. It even brought joy, so they had revelation and understanding. They must have even expected harvest for themselves.

But then the adversary, the devil, came as he did to the wayside people. Immediately, Satan was there to take the Word out of their hearts. He came to get the seed that prospers into harvest.

Satan can't just take the Word out of your heart. He doesn't have the authority to do that. He comes to tempt you, test you, lie to you until you let go of it. He tries to talk you into changing what you believe. He wants you to believe what he says instead of what God says.

Faith comes by hearing the Word (Romans 10:17). Unbelief comes by hearing also. Satan begins to bring pressure on you to let go of what God says in favor of the lie he is saying.

This situation reminds me of the time Abraham offered a sacrifice to the Lord, and he actually had to fight to keep the birds of prey from eating the sacrifice (Genesis 15:9-11)!

That's what you and I have to do with the Word of God. We have to fight the good fight of faith, standing on God's promises and resisting the devil when he comes to steal the Word that has been sown into our hearts.

The enemy will try to tell you, *It will never work—God isn't going to be faithful to His Word. God doesn't care anything about you.* That's when you have to put up your shield of faith and refuse to allow the devil to steal God's Word out of your heart. Don't let the devil get your Word seed. It will never become victory if you let Satan have it.

How long must you hold fast to God's Word and resist the devil's unbelief? As long as it takes. Hold fast until victory comes!

You see, the devil comes to steal the Word so he can regain control of your life. He wants to control your desires. He wants to control your money. He wants to control your family. His goal is to keep an open door into your life so he can come in to kill, steal and destroy.

But all the devil can do is talk to you. He has no power or authority over you. He has to talk you into giving up the authority you have over him in Christ. In fact, he tries to use your authority against you by causing you to agree with him instead of with God. He has no place in your life unless you give it to him.

However, even though a believer doesn't belong to the devil's domain any longer, that doesn't guarantee that he will stay free from the devil's control. That person has to gain understanding of how spiritual things work. He has to live by the principles of the kingdom of God. Otherwise, the devil will still be able to influence him to do what he wants.

Believers must receive and live by the revelation knowledge of God's Word in order to stay free from the devil's control. But, thank God, light and revelation are abounding in this day! This is an exciting time of God's light going forth, and it will get brighter and brighter from now on until we leave this earth.

It's easy to get into the stream of God's Spirit right now. But remember, the devil will try anything to keep you out of that supernatural stream. Stay alert to his attempts to steal the Word out of your heart. It doesn't bother him too much if the Word is in your head; he wants to keep it from abiding in your heart, where God's anointing abides and comes forth. Once the seed of God's Word has taken root in good ground, the devil knows he is in big trouble!

It's so wonderful to live by the truth of God's Word—to wake up in the morning and not be afraid. To know you have put yourself in the hands of the living God, Who never, never, never fails to keep His Word to you. To know that you can take hold of the words that He has already spoken in His Book, and they will assuredly come to pass!

All that is yours—if you don't let the devil talk you out of it! That's where the pressure of the faith fight is felt—in keeping the devil from stealing the Word.

So when the pressure is on and the devil is saying you're not going to receive your answer, don't yield to unbelief and lose your harvest. Remember, you are the one who is responsible for your spiritual growth. Be a fighter of the faith. Keep the fowls of the air from eating the Word seed sown into your heart!

OFFENSE UPROOTS YOUR WORD SEED

Talking you into offense is a major strategy Satan uses to get you to dig up your Word seed. Remember, the Word is now in your heart. Satan can't get it out himself. He has to convince you

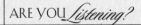

to cast the Word out of your heart. If he can get you offended, you will destroy your own harvest. When you become offended, you stumble and make false steps in life. *The Amplified Bible* gives a good illustration of this concerning those who have stony-ground hearts:

> **The ones sown upon stony ground are those who, when they hear the Word, at once receive and accept and welcome it with joy; And they have no real root in themselves, and so they endure for a little while; then when trouble or persecution arises on account of the Word, they immediately are offended (become displeased, indignant, resentful) and they stumble and fall away.**
>
> **(Mark 4:16-17)**

Jesus said in the parable the seed **"withered away"** (v. 6). When a person takes offense, immediately his spiritual walk begins to wither away. The flow of life from his spirit begins to ebb, and he begins to dry up inside. *The Amplified Bible* says **"they stumble and fall away"** (v. 17). Becoming offended is a stumbling block.

We don't ever have any business drying up on the inside. We are believers! We have the Word. Psalm 119:165 says, **"Great peace have they which love thy law: and nothing shall offend them."** As we continually feed our spirits with the Word and keep our roots strong and established, we gain the spiritual strength we need to avoid the enemy's strategy of offense altogether.

DON'T ALLOW OFFENSE IN YOUR LIFE

The basic problem with stony ground is that the Word is not rooted because the soil is shallow and full of rocks. Sometimes people get turned on to the Word of God and put it into motion in their lives. But six weeks later—when they don't see any difference in their situation—they become offended. Nothing has happened. No results. No return. No increase.

We have to be willing to make a stand that the Word of God is true, regardless of how things look and no matter how long it takes to manifest in the natural realm. After more than 32 years of experience, I can tell you this: A lot of times, it doesn't happen as soon as we want it to. And the number-one reason why it doesn't happen sooner is not God—it's you and me.

You may think, *It's been six weeks since I started believing for my healing, and I can't tell any difference in my body. God must not have heard me. He must not care anything about me.*

Be careful! You are offended, and you are thinking like stony ground! Don't let the devil talk you into being offended at God. *God is never your problem.*

If things aren't going right in our lives, we have to look at what we are doing. It is a total waste of time to blame it on God. He is full of compassion. He is always right, and He is always good. He always wants the best for us.

You will never catch God off the job. You will never find Him late. You will never find Him anything but merciful and eager to meet your needs, so don't take offense at Him.

When the devil can't cause us to take offense at God, he tries to cause us to become offended at the preacher who taught us the Word. The enemy whispers thoughts to our minds like, *That minister doesn't preach right! What he said doesn't work. That was all just talk!*

If you won't take offense at the preacher, the devil will then try to offend you through your spouse, your children, your

neighbor, your boss—anyone he can find! He wants to get you under his control again so he can put you back into poverty, bondage and sickness. He knows that strife, envy and offense are big open doors he can walk through to take over your life.

> **If ye have bitter envying and strife in your hearts, glory not, and lie not against the truth. This wisdom descendeth not from above, but is earthly, sensual, devilish. For where envying and strife is, there is confusion and every evil work.**
>
> **(James 3:14-16)**

You see, when you take offense at someone, your spiritual walk is immediately crippled. Your faith won't work, because faith works by love (Galatians 5:6). That puts you on dangerous ground. Mark 11:25 says that as long as you choose to stay offended, your Heavenly Father won't forgive you: **"When ye stand praying, forgive, if ye have ought against any: that your Father also which is in heaven may forgive you your trespasses."**

No matter what anyone does to you, it's never all right for you to be offended. Never. If you are offended, you are wrong! The other person who offended you may be in the wrong, too. But the moment you took offense, you became wrong as well.

So even if someone spits in your face, do what Jesus said to do: forgive. Refuse to let strife in. It is deadly.

It is especially important to walk in the love of God at home. Strife at home is one of Satan's major ploys. If Satan can stop you before you get out the front door, you will never be any trouble to him anywhere else.

It's amazing how many doors to the devil you will shut if you will simply walk according to 1 Corinthians 13. So make the quality decision not to allow offense in your life. Determine not to be touchy, fretful or resentful. Don't take account of an evil done to you (1 Corinthians 13:5). Plant 1 Corinthians 13:4-8 deeply in your heart. I like the *Amplified* translation:

Love endures long and is patient and kind; love never is envious nor boils over with jealousy, is not boastful or vainglorious, does not display itself haughtily.

It is not conceited (arrogant and inflated with pride); it is not rude (unmannerly), and does not act unbecomingly. Love (God's love in us) does not insist on its own rights or its own way, for it is not self-seeking; it is not touchy or fretful or resentful; it takes no account of the evil done to it [it pays no attention to a suffered wrong].

It does not rejoice at injustice and unrighteousness, but rejoices when right and truth prevail.

Love bears up under anything and everything that comes, is ever ready to believe the best of every person, its hopes are fadeless under all circumstances, and it endures everything [without weakening].

Love never fails [never fades out or becomes obsolete or comes to an end]. As for prophecy (the gift of inter-preting the divine will and purpose), it will be fulfilled and pass away; as for tongues, they will be destroyed and cease; as for knowledge, it will pass away [it will lose its value and be superseded by truth].

Let this rule your words and actions. Don't give offense a place to start. When you get out of love, immediately repent and make it right. Let go of past hurts and offenses that people have caused, and *refuse* to blame God for your problems.

Do you want to know the best way to keep from being offended? Stay on fire for God. Stay in the Word. Listen to good teaching tapes. Get in a good church that preaches the Word. Don't go to a church that is cold and dead, unless you want to end up the same way. Faith comes by hearing, but so does unbelief. Therefore, fellowship with people who are full of the Word of God, full of faith and full of the love of God.

You may say, "Well, there *is* no church like that where we live." Then start one! Or if you aren't called to start one, help someone else do it. Don't keep going to a church that drains you of faith every Sunday morning so that you have to go home to your teaching tapes and your Bible just to get back on track!

And don't decide, *This faith business must not work, because my answer didn't come as soon as I wanted it to.* If you keep thinking like that, you will join the group Jesus calls stony ground! They wouldn't stand when trouble came. When the devil came to steal the Word, they just let him have it. They became offended, lost their harvest and bore no fruit.

GET DEEPLY ROOTED IN THE WORD

So the first group of people had no understanding, but this second group had no roots. They didn't stay in the Word long enough to allow their roots to grow, so it was easy for Satan to steal the Word from them.

To grow strong roots, you have to dig deeply into the Word. Don't just let other people do your digging for you—you'll miss out on the best part! You have to dig into the Word yourself to receive the fullness of a revelation. All ministers can do is point the way for you to start your own treasure hunt. As you spend time in God's Word, The Holy Spirit will reveal to you exactly the understanding necessary for constant success and victory.

I guarantee you, time in the Word is time well spent. The Word of God is so rich—I just revel in it. I tangibly feel the presence of God more when I'm just studying and receiving insight into the Word than I do any other time. Jeremiah said that God's Word is a fire (Jeremiah 20:9). It's powerful. It's supernatural!

> **For the word of God is quick, and powerful, and sharper than any twoedged sword, piercing even to the dividing asunder of soul and spirit, and of the joints and marrow, and is a discerner of the thoughts and intents of the heart.**
>
> **(Hebrews 4:12)**

As you dig into the Word, don't expect to renew your mind and retrain your thinking overnight. It takes time. But the more you are faithful to spend time in the Word and in fellowship with God, the stronger the roots of God's Word will grow inside of you and the more impossible it will be for the devil to pressure you into giving in to unbelief. You will become like a tree planted by streams of water. Your roots will be so deep and strong that the devil will never be able to pull the Word of God out of your heart.

> **Blessed is the man that walketh not in the counsel of the ungodly, nor standeth in the way of sinners, nor sitteth in the seat of the scornful. But his delight is in the law of the Lord; and in his law doth he meditate day and night. And he shall be like a tree planted by the rivers of water, that bringeth forth his fruit in his**

season; his leaf also shall not wither; and whatsoever
he doeth shall prosper.

(Psalm 1:1-3)

It's so important to keep moving once you start walking by
faith. Walk in the light you have, but keep going after more
light. You have to guard that "Word garden" planted in your
heart. You can never stop fighting the good fight of faith. Satan
will continue to try to steal the Word out of your heart. You just
have to continue to refuse to let him have it!

Constantly feed on God's Word to keep the Word in the
midst of your heart. Proverbs 4 says to attend to the Word,
incline your ear, keep it in front of your eyes. This is God's
prescription for getting His Word into your heart. That is the
only way your roots will remain strong and your thoughts and
your words will stay in line with God's ways. Then the enemy
won't be able to find a way to get you back into his lowlife,
defeated system of calamity.

THE THORNY GROUND

Jesus goes on to describe the third group of people, repre-
sented by the thorny ground:

And these are they which are sown among thorns;
such as hear the word, And the cares of this world, and
the deceitfulness of riches, and the lusts of other things
entering in, choke the word, and it becometh unfruitful.

(Mark 4:18-19)

The person whom Jesus calls "thorny ground" actually has
the seed of the Word sown into his heart. However, his heart is

overcrowded with the cares of this world, the deceitfulness of riches and the lust for other things. These other things have cluttered the person's heart so much that they have choked the Word and made it unproductive.

I once heard a minister teach about cluttered hearts. He asked the congregation, "Do you have one of those closets where you put everything but can't find anything?"

I confess—I have a room like that in my house. It's called an exercise room, but that's in name only. A person can hardly walk through that room, much less do a sit-up or a jumping jack! Boxes and all kinds of things are stacked in there. The only exercise anyone could get in my "exercise room" is to dig his way through all the stuff from the front of the room to the back!

I have no idea anymore what all is in that room. Sometimes I go in there looking for something, and I'll think, *Where did that come from? What is that doing here?* There is so much stuff in there. I'm determined to get in that room and clean it up—but not today!

That "exercise room" is a picture of some people's hearts. These people have so much junk in their hearts, they can't even draw on the Word they once planted there. There's too much other stuff, and it chokes the Word as weeds will choke your garden.

The Bible says, **"Love not the world, neither the things that are in the world"** (1 John 2:15). Desire for God and His kingdom is what belongs in our hearts—not the other things of this world that clamor for our time and attention. There are pleasures in this life, and the Father wants each of us to enjoy the good that He has put in the earth for us. But those things are not for the heart. God and His kingdom—including family, church, calling, obedience—these are for the heart.

It is easy in a busy world to get our priorities out of order. If we're not careful, that can happen to us. We can become so caught up in the cares of daily life that we don't make time for God and His kingdom to be first place. Our lives become busier and busier with the cares and concerns of family, work, errands, chores, hobbies, sports and leisure activities—until, finally, we don't have sufficient time to fellowship with God.

The cares and distractions that choke the Word in people's lives are what Jesus called "thorns." The people who have thorny ground in their hearts receive the same return on their seed as the ground by the wayside and the stony ground: nothing. They bear no fruit and receive no harvest.

I think *The Amplified Bible* gives more insight into the overcrowded heart.

> **The ones sown among the thorns are others who hear the Word; Then the cares and anxieties of the world and distractions of the age, and the pleasure and delight and false glamour and deceitfulness of riches, and the craving and passionate desire for other things creep in and choke and suffocate the Word, and it becomes fruitless.**
>
> **(Mark 4:18-19)**

Cares and anxieties of this world! How easy it is to yield to worry. That's why Philippians 4:6 says, **"Do not fret or have any anxiety about anything"** (AMP).

You see, money and things are not all that can clutter your heart. Worry can take you over. A believer should never worry. He should pray always, Paul wrote in his letter, and with thanksgiving make his requests to God and then let the peace of God take over.

When care and worry come, pray based on what God has already said is His will for you—get specific promises to stand on. Believe God's Word. Rebuke worry—which is unbelief. Don't meditate on the problem. Meditate on the answer—God's Word. Act in faith and speak in faith!

If watching the news puts care, fear, worry into you, don't feed on it. Spend that time in the "good news"—that's what the word *gospel* means. A preacher friend of mine said, because he hadn't watched the news, "You've been through several crises I didn't know anything about!"

In our day you can watch bad news 24 hours a day, but that doesn't mean you should!

What age has ever had as many distractions as this one? There is constant noise—TV, radios, videotapes, audiotapes, CDs, telephones, computers, movies, sports of all kinds. There are all kinds of hobbies, not to mention that in our generation all kinds of sin are highly developed and well marketed. Pleasure and false glamour abound and so many "things" to want. One fad after another. All of these distractions lead to the big one—deceitfulness of riches! There is the love of money that is Satan's root (1 Timothy 6:10). Money is for using and money is for giving, but money is not for loving!

In fact, money makes a very poor god. You can own the whole world with a ribbon tied around it. But if you don't have God, you are not a happy camper. Something is desperately wrong in your life—something money won't fix. Instead, money will help you go to hell faster if you don't honor God with it.

That's one of the reasons tithing is so wonderful. Giving God the best and the first of your increase helps to keep you free from the love of money so that you can handle money without it affecting your faithfulness to God.

Make sure you seek God first (Matthew 6:33). Don't let anything else be first in your life above God. Don't even let something else be on the same level as God.

I'm not just talking about things that are sin. You have to demand everything in your life comes under the dominion of God and His Word—even necessary things, such as your career. Refuse to let your heart be overcome by anything.

THE MOST IMPORTANT THING: YOUR HEART

It doesn't matter if you operate the biggest business in the world; the most important thing in your life is your heart. Keeping your spirit full of the Word of God is the most vital responsibility you have. A heart full of the Word makes everything else come out right. So give God and His Word first place in your heart.

I have found that the best thing I can do to keep God first in my heart is to spend time fellowshiping with Him every morning before I do anything else. Making that a habit has helped me keep my heart from becoming cluttered with anything that could take over my time and attention. I've learned that it helps keep your priorities in order and your life in agreement with God's desires for you (always the highest and best possible).

It's important that you make a quality decision to spend time with God, because it is easy to spend your time on other things and lose your desire for the Word of God. As you begin to focus your time and attention on the new project or activity, your regular time spent in the Word falls off, and your desire for the things of God drains away.

I want to avoid that happening in my life at all costs, so every day I spend time with God in prayer. I don't spend time in the Word every morning, though that is my preference. But I do start my day fellowshiping with the Lord. That morning time with the Father has really changed me. I mean that literally. I am so different spiritually now from what I was. Some people say, "Well, you don't really need to do that. You don't want to be under bondage."

Listen, I'm not under any bondage. I decided in 1983 that the first thing I would do every day for the rest of my life is spend time with God. It's the best investment of time I have ever made. It's the way I keep myself steady and straight in my spiritual walk.

At the time of this writing, Kenneth and I are in the process of building a home. I prayed a long time about whether or not to build this home, because I knew it would take a lot of my time. I wanted to be sure it was in God's plan, and I wanted to be sure that building a house wouldn't clutter up my heart. I knew that the amount of time expended on the project was an even more important consideration than the money it would cost. I didn't want to get pulled away from honoring God first with my time and attention.

After we made the decision to go ahead with the project, I made up my mind, *I'm not going to get carried away with this home and spend more time on it than I should.* Even the planning of this home has been a slow process because I would not give more of myself to it than I could spiritually afford. It can't be first place. I've honored the Lord in it and He has blessed me. I have kept my heart from being cluttered with concerns about it, and He is giving me a house free from clutter. (Yes, this new house will have an exercise room with exercise equipment—not stuff!) I will not give myself to anything in this life except the Lord!

Your desire follows your attention. Wherever you give your attention is where your desire will be. As you keep your heart turned toward God, your desire will stay turned toward Him as well. If you think you don't have the love for God that you should, give Him more attention. Spend your vacation with us in a Believers' Convention and do nothing but God for six days. You will never be the same. One word from God will change your life forever!

So keep your heart centered on God. Don't let anything else take over your thought life and usurp His place in your heart. A life tightly centered on Him is the only one worth living!

"Keep thy heart with all diligence; for out of it are the issues of life" (Proverbs 4:23).

THE GOOD GROUND

Finally, Jesus talked about the good ground—the only group of people that actually enjoyed harvest.

> **And those sown on the good (well-adapted) soil are the ones who hear the Word and receive and accept and welcome it and bear fruit—some thirty times as much as was sown, some sixty times as much, and some [even] a hundred times as much.**
>
> **(Mark 4:20, AMP)**

> **But he that received seed into the good ground is he that heareth the word, and understandeth it; which also beareth fruit, and bringeth forth, some an hundredfold, some sixty, some thirty.**
>
> **(Matthew 13:23)**

Jesus said the heart that is good ground hears, receives, accepts and welcomes the Word that is heard. Matthew tells us the Word is received by hearing with understanding. This is very important insight. Revelation by the Holy Spirit must accompany the hearing to bear fruit.

There's another important factor, however, that allows the good ground to bear fruit. **"But that on the good ground are they, which in an honest and good heart, having heard the word, keep it, and bring forth fruit with patience"** (Luke 8:15).

We learn from Luke that good ground hears the Word, latches on to it and won't let go of it, no matter what. A heart that receives manifestation is a patient heart. **"Be not slothful, but followers of them who through faith and patience inherit the promises.... And so, after he** [Abraham] **had patiently endured, he obtained the promise"** (Hebrews 6:12, 15). This kind of ground produces a crop—some thirty, some sixty and some a hundredfold.

Good ground hears, understands and holds on to the Word until it produces harvest. That agrees with what Jesus said in John 15. There He taught that it is the abiding or indwelling Word that accomplishes whatever you ask.

What kind of ground do *you* want to be? It's your choice, but let me encourage you—determine within yourself to be good ground. Be quick to hear. Look to the Holy Spirit for revelation. When you see something in the Word of God, hear it and do it. Let it change your will. Let it change your mind. Let it change your actions.

Don't just hear the parts you want to hear. For instance, don't just hear the promises about prosperity and not the directions for living holy before God. You can't take the blessing part without the obedience part. The kingdom of God doesn't operate that way. You have to honor God by obeying *all* His Word. The blessing comes on you as you obey God's wisdom—His way of doing things. Blessing is the result of hearing God and obeying Him.

Making your heart good ground for the seed of the Word by hearing and doing is the key to life. The Word of God in your heart concerning healing will bring healing to your body. The Word of God in your heart concerning prosperity will bring abundance to your finances. Whatever you need, you will find the answer in God's Word. But it is how you hear the Word and obey in that area that will determine your increase.

Prayer of Consecration

Dear Father, I commit myself to Your Word. I put Your Word first place in my life. I know You and I honor Your Word. As I spend time with You in Your Word, give me understanding and revelation. I make the quality decision to be good ground and retain Your Word. I refuse to let the devil steal the Word out of my heart. I refuse to compromise. I will not let go of the Word regardless of circumstances. I'm not moved by what I see but by what You say! I will let patience have her perfect work, so I believe for full harvest and I expect to receive. Thank You for Your Word that is given to me as seed for blessing in my life.

THINK ON THESE THINGS

*We are to be witnesses to the manifested kingdom
of God—not only with our mouths, but with our lives.*

*Believers must receive and live by the revelation knowledge
of God's Word in order to stay free from the devil's control.*

*You will never catch God off the job. You will
never find Him late. You will never find Him
anything but merciful and eager to meet your needs.*

*The more you are faithful to spend time in the Word
and in fellowship with God, the stronger the
roots of God's Word will grow inside of you.*

Wherever you give your attention is where your desire will be.

*Making your heart good ground for the seed of
the Word by hearing and doing is the key to life.*

CHAPTER 13

PLANT THE
WORD...HARVEST
THE VICTORY

I n His teaching on how God's kingdom is manifested in the earth, Jesus does not stop with telling us only how to be good ground. He has more to say about what we are to do once the seed is planted to make sure we eventually reap our harvests.

BE CAREFUL WHAT YOU HEAR

Right after explaining the parable of the sower, Jesus makes a summary statement about the vital principle He has just taught:

And He said to them, Be careful what you are hearing. The measure [of thought and study] you give [to the truth you hear] will be the measure [of virtue and knowledge] that comes back to you—and more [besides] will be given to you who hear.

(Mark 4:24, AMP)

Your harvest depends on how you hear. Results from the Word of God are measured by the attention you give to the Word you hear. *The measure of honor and attention you give to the Word that you hear is the measure of power and virtue that will come into*

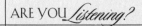

your heart to bring that Word to pass. **"So then faith cometh by hearing, and hearing by the word of God"** (Romans 10:17).

It is not the amount of Word you hear that determines your results. It's how much Word you hear with revelation or understanding. You receive more reading one chapter of the Bible with revelation than you would by reading the whole Bible and letting it go in one ear and out the other. Read the Bible with the reality of the truth that it is God speaking to you and with the intent to do what He says.

In my own private Bible studies, I usually read a passage of Scripture first in the *King James Version.* Then I often look through Bullinger's *Companion Bible*[1] to see what his notes say, and I also read the *Amplified* version of the passage. I try to glean all I can out of what I'm reading. When I study the Word like that, it's wonderful to discover how much insight comes.

The next time you study that same scripture, you'll probably see things you didn't see the last time you paid attention to it. If we don't pay close attention to the Word of God, or if we just pick out the parts we like, it's easy to miss the light that God wants us to have. On the other hand, when our attitude about the Word is "I hear it, I receive it, I act on it and I will not let the devil take it away from me!" we allow the power and virtue in the Word of God to change our lives. That is when it bears fruit in our lives.

That's why Jesus warns, **"Be careful what you are hearing."** The way into your heart is by giving attention with your eyes and your ears (Proverbs 4:20-21). You can't do that without giving your time to it.

---

[1] *The Companion Bible* (Grand Rapids: Kregel Publications, 1990).

It's not only important how you hear but what you hear. For instance, suppose you go to faith conventions once a year and then attend a church that preaches unbelief for the other 51 weeks of the year. You can't expect to grow strong in faith like that because unbelief comes by hearing also. You have to be careful what you let into your heart through your ears and your eyes.

You can see why Kenneth and I put so much emphasis on the Word of God in our teaching. People call us Word people, and they don't always mean that as a compliment. But it is a compliment.

People can never insult Ken and me by calling us Word people. We honor the Word as God speaking to us right now. That's what makes the Word so alive to us. If it were just something to study to learn mental knowledge, it wouldn't be life to us, and it would never have transformed our lives.

The Bible says that the Word is quick and alive and more powerful than any two-edged sword (Hebrews 4:12). *The Amplified Bible* says it this way:

The Word that God speaks is alive and full of power [making it active, operative, energizing and effective]; it is sharper than any two-edged sword, penetrating to the dividing line of the breath of life (soul) and [the immortal] spirit, and of joints and marrow [of the deepest parts of our nature], exposing and sifting and analyzing and judging the very thoughts and purposes of the heart.

These creative words come out of God's mouth in His power. His power is still in His words. The words of God are creative power. They have been written down for you and me so we can put them before our eyes and into our ears. And Ken and I have proven in our own experience for more than 32 years that as we plant God's words in the midst of our hearts, those words come forth in His power and anointing to accomplish the results promised.

So don't hear the Word and think, *Well, that sounds good, but it won't work for me. I don't deserve it.* You won't release any power or virtue into your life from that kind of response to the Word, because you disqualified yourself.

Instead of talking yourself out of what is available, not because you deserve it but because Jesus purchased it for you, do this: Find a scripture that promises you something, such as, "By His stripes, I am healed" (Isaiah 53:5, author's paraphrase). Then grab hold of it: "That's for me! I am healed. No sickness or disease can stay in my body." If you aren't right with God, get right by repenting and receiving your forgiveness. Repenting includes going in another direction. When you repent, you turn from sin and go God's way.

Receive the Word of God as truth and let it change your thinking and speaking. As you do, faith will arise in your heart, and God's power will come on the scene!

HOW THE WORD CHANGED OUR THINKING

Years ago Ken and I received the revelation that the Bible is the answer and that its words are supernatural and alive. We listened to Kenneth Hagin's teaching on the authority of the Word, and it got into our hearts.

We weren't theological students. We didn't try to dismantle and analyze every word we heard. We were just people who needed help. So when we heard the Word of God, we believed it and let it change our thinking. We made the commitment to do what the Word says, whether it was easy or hard.

You would be surprised to find out how many things that one decision cuts out of your life and how many temptations it overcomes. It makes your life so simple! For instance, you may think, *Maybe it would be better for me to tell a little lie in this situation.* Then you realize that you can't tell that little lie because you would be violating the Word of God that says you shall not lie (Exodus 20:16).

You know, God tells you and me what to do because He wants to make us free. His way works! His ways are higher than the world's ways and they produce life and blessing. Those who follow after the world lie, connive and sin—and then they receive the payoff—death. The Bible says that the wages of sin is death. God doesn't want us to live in death and calamity. He wants us to live out our full number of days in peace and righteousness and joy in the Holy Ghost. That is so much better than the turmoil, strife, fear, doubt, sickness and lack that the world offers!

When Ken and I first began to let the Word change our thinking, we were not prosperous on the outside at all. I mean, I had holes in my shoes when Ken started preaching prosperity! But we received the revelation of prosperity into our hearts, and we held fast to that revelation until it took over our natural circumstances.

We found that prosperity begins in your heart as you receive revelation of God's truth. Then that word of truth and faith will prosper you in the natural realm. **"Beloved, I pray that you may prosper in every way and [that your body] may keep well, even as [I know] your soul keeps well and prospers.... I have no greater joy than this, to hear that my [spiritual] children are living their lives in the Truth"** (3 John 2, 4, AMP).

Jesus said this to those who believed:

> When ye have lifted up the Son of man, then shall
> ye know that I am he, and that I do nothing of myself;
> but as my Father hath taught me, I speak these things.
> And he that sent me is with me: the Father hath not
> left me alone; for I do always those things that please
> him. As he spake these words, many believed on him.
> Then said Jesus to those Jews which believed on him, If
> ye continue in my word, then are ye my disciples indeed;
> And ye shall know the truth, and the truth shall make
> you free.
>
> (John 8:29-32)

What Ken and I experienced was that freedom didn't happen
in our circumstances in a day. First it happened on the inside
and continued to increase. Then, as a result, our outer circumstances began to change from bondage to freedom. We are free
today inside and outside. To God be all the glory!

The years have come and gone, and Ken and I are still holding
fast to our commitment to obey the Word of God. God has never
disappointed us. His Word continues to grow in us and to work
for us as we continue to hear it, receive it and do it.

THE LIGHT OF REVELATION

> And He said to them, Is the lamp brought in to be
> put under a peck measure or under a bed, and not [to
> be put] on the lampstand? [Things are hidden temporar-
> ily only as a means to revelation.] For there is nothing
> hidden except to be revealed, nor is anything [temporar-
> ily] kept secret except in order that it may be made known.
>
> (Mark 4:21-22, AMP)

Jesus is talking about receiving revelation from God in this scripture. According to Proverbs 20:27, your spirit is the candle of the Lord. God lights your spirit with revelation of the Word. **"Thy word is a lamp unto my feet, and a light unto my path"** (Psalm 119:105).

I know exactly what that is like. I remember when Ken and I first heard it was God's will to prosper us. At the time, we were walking in such poverty and lack. But when we heard that truth, we began to leave defeat and come into victory. We began to *see* things in a different light—in God's light. We didn't pass over from lack into abundance when the money was actually manifested; we passed over when the light of revelation ignited in our hearts! The light of God in our hearts directing our path on the outside changed our entire lives to be able to experience the life God always wanted us to have. We were not waiting on Him; He was waiting on us to obey what He had already written in His Word!

Sometimes in my morning devotions, the light of revelation will go off on the inside of me as I sit alone in my quiet, little spot reading the Bible. I'll think, *Oh, dear God, that's the answer! I see that.* Other times I receive a divine correction that also is a great blessing, because I know God is showing me something that has been causing me problems—something I'm doing that is hindering God's best for me.

"For the grace of God (His unmerited favor and blessing) has come forward (appeared) for the deliverance from sin and the eternal salvation for all mankind. It has trained us to reject and renounce all ungodliness..." (Titus 2:11-12, AMP). It is the favor of God when He corrects us. His correction is always for our good.

There is no greater miracle on earth than what happens in your heart when your candle is lighted and you see in your spirit what God is saying to you. I have learned through the years that *when you get a revelation in your heart, you can walk it out in your life.* When that big explosion of insight, clarity, faith and power happens on the inside, the manifestation of your answer is as good as done—if you act on what you have heard.

When light comes, faith is there. You see, once the light comes into your spirit, and you walk out that revelation, it will prevail in your life.

You were born again to walk in the light. You can walk in such a place with God that you don't have to wonder or fear. You don't ever have to be in the dark about anything, because the Holy Spirit dwells in you to enlighten you.

All you have to do is keep God first place in your life and let your heart dominate your soul and your body. Then as you walk in the light you receive, you will see the kingdom of heaven manifested on every hand!

PLANTING AND HARVESTING IN THE KINGDOM OF GOD

So is the kingdom of God, as if a man should cast seed into the ground. And should sleep, and rise night and day, and the seed should spring and grow up, he knoweth not how. For the earth bringeth forth fruit of herself; first the blade, then the ear, after that the full corn in the ear. But when the fruit is brought forth, immediately he putteth in the sickle, because the harvest is come.

(Mark 4:26-29)

Jesus is teaching us how the spiritual kingdom of God is manifested in this natural realm. He is still teaching about the sower sows the Word. We already know that the seed is the Word of God and the ground is the heart of man. As a man casts the natural seed into the ground, so a person casts "Word seed" into the ground of his heart. He goes to bed and gets up. He can't see anything happening, but something is happening. The heart is processing the Word the same way the earth processes a natural seed. The earth knows what to do with seed. It is made to process seed!

Just so, your heart knows what to do with the Word. You sow it in there and the heart will process or accomplish the harvest (Isaiah 55:11)! It will bring forth any promise of God into your life.

So you sow the Word into your heart. You continue to water the Word and keep it alive by speaking it with your mouth, hearing it with your ears and reading it with your eyes. You listen to teaching tapes. You spend time in the Word.

As you continually give attention to the Word of God, your voice will begin to speak His Word that is already full of His power and bring substance or manifestation. The kingdom of God rises up in you to take hold and manifest your answer.

You may not see results for a while, but neither did the man in the parable. He planted the seed, went to sleep at night and got up day after day, and he didn't see even one sprig breaking the surface of the soil. Yet he didn't dig up his seed to see if it was working. He understood that the law of sowing seeds and reaping harvest takes time.

So over the next few weeks, he did his part. He couldn't see what was happening in the ground, but he knew from experience that the seed was growing underneath the surface. If that seed was watered and not destroyed or dug up, there would come a day when a blade would come into sight. If the blade was nurtured, an ear would be manifested and then the full corn in the ear.

NURTURING THE SEED PLANTED

You and I are the sowers. Our heart is the ground. Like this man in the parable, we have to do our part as well with the seed of the Word planted in our hearts. We nurture it, protect it, meditate on it, speak it. As we do, something starts happening in the ground of our hearts. Faith begins to grow even though we see no change in the natural.

This is the most difficult time to stay in faith—between the time you believe and the time you begin to see your answer. You have planted the seed of the Word, but it is still hidden from sight, working in the realm of the spirit.

As the earth knows exactly what to do with the seed, so the heart knows how to process the Word. When doubt tries to come, just say, "My heart is processing the Word of God concerning that. I'll not let it go!"

That is what walking by faith is all about. You have to choose to believe what God has said rather than what the devil or the circumstances or the symptoms say. You say what God says! You don't know how God will fulfill the promise of the Word you have planted. It may even be impossible in the natural. But you are walking by faith and not by sight, and all things are possible to you when you believe (2 Corinthians 5:7; Mark 9:23).

Remember, the seed has to grow down before it grows up. So you keep on feeding your heart the Word of God. You water the

Word in your heart with your confession of faith. You use your authority to keep the enemy away from the seed. And the Word begins to take root in your heart.

Your heart is God's garden. First Corinthians 3:6-7 reveals that you plant and water with His Word and it's God Who gives the increase. (By the way, this chapter teaches us more about Satan's major tools to get you to dig up your own seed. They are strife, envy, divisions. We have to avoid these traps and stay in love if we want harvest!)

FIRST THE BLADE, THEN THE EAR

This is the secret of the manifestation of God's kingdom. We cast the seed of God's Word into our hearts, and the seed begins to grow on the inside of us. Finally, the crop grows so big that it has to manifest outside our hearts against the circumstances.

We don't know how the heart is able to receive the Word, process it by faith and then cause it to come forth in power to change circumstances. We just know it is God's Word and God's power at work. We can't see the Word down in our spirits bringing things to pass. All we know is that God made it to work that way. The natural realm has been made subject to the realm of the spirit.

Let's look at Mark 4:28 again: **"For the earth bringeth forth fruit of herself; first the blade, then the ear, after that the full corn in the ear."** What is Jesus talking about? Harvest time. The ground of the heart has received and nurtured the seed of the Word. Now it begins to bring forth fruit of itself.

That fruit is the Anointing of God. The heart brings forth the Word of God by that anointing or power and applies it to sickness, lack and any other problem that hinders our increase in life.

Our part is to keep the Word planted in good soil that is enriched with faith and understanding.

We can do that. We can have that much confidence in God. We can trust Him even in the hard places. We can do our part.

The Anointing of God will work in your affairs as you keep the seed planted in your heart and in your mouth. **Faith has to be in two places—in your heart and in your mouth** (Mark 11:23; Romans 10:9-10).

First the blade.

You begin to see a little change. You keep walking through your daily life, all the while protecting your seed: "Devil, you will not steal the Word out of my heart. In the Name of Jesus, I'm telling you that my God shall supply all my need according to His riches in Christ Jesus (Philippians 4:19). Devil, I cast you out. You cannot have that seed!"

Then the ear.

All of a sudden, you see a little sprig coming up. You get some relief. There is a change in your circumstances. Some unexpected finances come in to pay a bill that is due. The symptoms begin to disappear in your body. You begin to see with your eyes in the natural realm what has been happening all along in the spiritual realm.

Your blade is growing into a stalk. You didn't let the devil steal your seed, and now something is happening in the natural realm that you can see with your natural eyes.

But now you surely can't quit! You may have to look at that little sprig for a while but, thank God, you have a sprig to look at!

Just keep protecting your crop: "Devil, don't you even think about squashing this sprig! I refuse to listen to you. I have authority over you, and I command you, in the Name of Jesus, to get out of my sight! You cannot have God's Word that is planted in my heart. I determine what happens to the seed in my heart, and I'm telling you, you can't have it!" As you do this, keep saying with your mouth what you have received in your heart. Call things that be not as though they were. That is the spirit of faith. They already are in the spirit, though not yet in the natural. By saying what you believe, you are bringing into manifestation those desires that you believed you received when you prayed (Romans 4:16-21; 2 Corinthians 4:13; Mark 11:24).

After that the full corn in the ear.

That is essentially what you have to do to receive the rest of your harvest. Keep standing in faith. Don't quit when you see the sprig. Don't quit when you see the stalk. Keep walking by faith until the full harvest comes, no matter how long it takes. As you do, all the devils in hell, all the governments that man can put together, all the situations that could ever come against you in this life will have to bow their knees to the Word of the living God. It is a supernatural seed that overcomes all obstacles.

"But it's been four years now that I've been believing for a new house." Stay with it. **Don't give up. Double up!** Double up on the time and attention that you give to the Word of God. Double up on your saying of what you desire in your heart to come to pass. Jesus taught you how in Mark 11:23-24. You can do it!

When I first started learning to walk by faith, I believed God for six years to pay cash for a new home. Where would I be today if I hadn't continued to stand during those six years? I still wouldn't have a house. Psalm 27:13-14 says, **"[What, what would have become of me] had I not believed that I would see the Lord's goodness in the land of the living! Wait and hope for and**

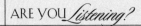

expect the Lord; be brave and of good courage and let your heart be stout and enduring. Yes, wait for and hope for and expect the Lord" (AMP).

Where will you be this time next year or 10 years from now if you don't believe the Word of God concerning the needs in your life? Right where you are today or maybe further away from your answer.

If you want a change, make a change. Put God's Word first place. Believe it. Live by it. Live on the victory side!

God has given you and me everything it takes to live by faith and be victorious. He has given us a new heart in which to grow and process the supernatural seed of the Word. He has given us His Spirit to strengthen us, teach us, give us light day by day and keep us walking in victory. There is no reason whatsoever for us to be defeated in life.

But remember, Luke 8:15 says we have to bring forth our fruit with patience. We might not receive our answer in a day or a week or a month. At first we may only see the blade. It may be much later that we see the ear. But no matter how long it takes for our harvest to come to fruition, we can't give in or quit. If we don't believe, we know there will be no harvest ever. But as we are faithful to water the seed with our faith, the day will come when the fruit is brought forth, and we will receive **"the full corn in the ear."** The kingdom of God will be manifested and made substance that we can eat, wear, drive, live in and enjoy. On that day, we will rejoice as we reap our harvest!

AS A GRAIN OF MUSTARD SEED

Up to this point, Jesus has shared several secrets of God's kingdom to teach us how to receive a harvest for anything we need in life. In Mark 4:30-32, He gives us another secret of the kingdom:

And he said, Whereunto shall we liken the kingdom of God? or with what comparison shall we compare it? It is like a grain of mustard seed, which, when it is sown in the earth, is less than all the seeds that be in the earth: But when it is sown, it groweth up, and becometh greater than all herbs, and shooteth out great branches; so that the fowls of the air may lodge under the shadow of it.

A mustard seed is so small that you can hardly see it. But when you plant it in the ground, that seed eventually grows into a tree that is large enough for birds to make their homes in its branches.

In the same way, the seed of God's dominion in your life can seem so little in the beginning. But if it is watered and tended to and nourished—if it is talked and believed and depended on—it grows up to become greater than any problem you could ever face. That tiny seed will eventually bring forth such a mighty harvest that the desire of your heart is fulfilled.

That was true for Ken and me. When we started believing God to get out of debt, the Word we planted in our hearts seemed so small compared to the financial disaster in which we lived.

I mean, we were in need of just about everything. We had no success in life. We didn't know how to handle our lives and make things work for us. We didn't have the house, clothes or money we needed. We didn't have the wisdom we needed. We didn't know what to do next.

All the problems we faced seemed so big, so impossible. For example, we needed a good car. But buying a new car seemed

impossible. To top it all off, we were being sued over a washer and dryer, and we were behind on other payments. Now, the worst the company could do to us was come and repossess those appliances, but the whole situation seemed so overwhelming to us.

So we started planting those little seeds of the Word and little seeds of money (we only had little seeds of both). Over a period of time the dominion of God just kept getting bigger and bigger on the inside of us. Then it began to manifest on the outside. Over the next 11 months, it brought forth a new car and paid off our debts. We rented a nice house and later paid cash for our first house. All the while, our Word seed was growing and our money seed was growing. We were sowing and reaping. Our needs got bigger and our seeds got bigger, and the Word got bigger in our hearts.

And this process of growing never ends. The kingdom of God just keeps getting bigger and bigger in our hearts. No matter what God tells us to do in the future or how impossible it seems, Ken and I know the harvest will be there to accomplish it if we will be as the man who cast seed into the ground. We know how to manifest the kingdom of God in the earth.

Whatever your need is, it isn't too big for God. He isn't limited by anything except your refusal to do things His way. The greater your faith, the more pleasure you give the Father. Without faith it's impossible to please God (Hebrews 11:6). With faith He is pleased! After all, that's exactly what He has been trying to get His people to do for generations—to hear and obey what He says so He can prosper them.

THE POWER IN A SEED

The Word of God will grow up to become anything right and good in your life for which you have the spiritual courage to stand. God's anointing will work in your spirit and empower your words, causing you to overcome every problem, no matter how impossible it looks.

For instance, suppose cancer is ravaging a person's body. His body is weak and close to death. But he takes the Word of God concerning healing and plants it in his heart. That seed seems so small and insignificant compared to a terminal disease. But it isn't insignificant. Even the smallest seed of God's Word is full of power! And as that person refuses to let it go, that seed will grow up to manifest victory in his body.

Recently I heard a man's testimony in Healing School concerning this very situation. He was dying of cancer. He got hold of the Healing School tapes. These are messages about what God's will is for your wholeness. He said he started planting that Word in his heart, and today he is well and cancer free. It works! To God be the glory!

You see, when you start planting that powerful seed in your heart and speaking God's Word out of your mouth, there isn't a cancer in the world that can stay in your body. There isn't a poverty devil in this world that can keep you in lack. Those little seeds grow up to become so great and powerful and mighty in your heart that they establish the kingdom and dominion of Almighty God Himself in your life.

Just think about that natural, little mustard seed. It has the power in it to duplicate itself and to grow up to become a mighty tree. That should help you comprehend the power hidden within the seed of God's Word.

Isaiah 55:10-11 gives us a clue regarding just how powerful this divine seed is:

> For as the rain cometh down, and the snow from
> heaven, and returneth not thither, but watereth the
> earth, and maketh it bring forth and bud, that it may
> give seed to the sower, and bread to the eater: So shall
> my word be that goeth forth out of my mouth: it shall
> not return unto me void, but it shall accomplish that
> which I please, and it shall prosper in the thing whereto
> I sent it.

There is no situation you face that the Word of God cannot solve or change. But first the seed of the Word must be planted in your heart, then you must speak it into your situation in faith. As that Word goes forth in power, it accomplishes that which God pleases and never returns unto Him void, because God's Word has His power in it to cause itself to come to pass.

When you stand steadfast in faith in a given situation, God's Word will come to pass and prosper in the purpose for which He sent it. If it's a Word seed about healing, it prospers in a harvest of healing. If it's a Word seed about finances, it prospers in a harvest of abundance and increase. God established it that way in the beginning when He said, "Every seed will produce after its own kind" (Genesis 1:12). God's Word has gone out of His mouth to give us the seed to meet any need!

Jesus' words in John 15:7 also show us how powerful God's Word is: **"If ye abide in me, and my words abide in you, ye shall ask what ye will, and it shall be done unto you."** When the seed of God's supernatural Word abides, remains and dwells in your heart, whatever you ask the Father, in Jesus' Name, shall come to pass.

But you have to keep planting that Word in your heart until there is more Word in there than anything else. And it must be watered and given time to grow properly. You nurture it, water it, say it with your mouth and refuse to let the devil steal those words out of your heart. Keep them protected by your decision that "I believe the Word of God, and I'm not going to change. I won't back out on it. The devil is not going to steal from me because he can't talk me out of it." Then it will grow up and become harvest for you. One day you'll put in the sickle and that house will be there, that car will be there, that healing you're believing for will be there. The Word of God will grow up and become whatever it says, when it's planted and allowed to grow to maturity. That is the secret of how the kingdom of God is manifested in your life.

KEEP ON PLANTING

Once your harvest is manifested, what do you do then? You continue in the Word. You don't quit planting, and you don't quit growing. You continually plant the Word in your heart so you can continually reap a harvest of dominion and victory in your life.

You see, a farmer has to go out every year and plant a field of new seed in order to reap a new crop. But you and I have no such limitations. We have been born again to be a depository of God's Word. God created us to plant seed and reap a continual crop of victory every single day of our lives. We can do it indefinitely. There is certainly no lack of ground. Our spirit man has no fences, no limitations.

The amount you decide to plant is the size your harvest will be. It's up to you. God has always worked that way. He doesn't tell you to do anything impossible, but He does tell you what to do.

So if you want to be a spiritual giant, first be a person who casts the Word into his heart continually. Your spirit man will begin to take dominion in your life over your body, over your affairs and over your thinking. Instead of living like a carnal person, you will live in a continual feast of joy and peace in the kingdom of God.

Never let yourself get stagnant in your spiritual walk. You have to keep growing and developing. Otherwise, you will start going backward. You just can't stay in one place spiritually if you want continual harvest.

As we keep on planting God's Word in the ground of our hearts, more and more dominion will rise up out of our hearts to manifest in our lives.

We are the sons and daughters of God in the earth, and we are in the process of coming into full spiritual maturity. Our goal is to fully preach this gospel to every nation before the end comes. That takes money. It takes power. It takes anointing. But it all starts with a seed—the Word of God.

Every great ministry that has ever been born into the earth started with the seed of God's Word planted in someone's heart. As each person nurtured that seed with his diligence and faith, that seed then took root and grew up to become the kingdom of God in manifestation on the earth, revealing the goodness of God as a witness.

Whatever you need and whatever God has called you to do in life, it all goes right back to this parable. A man casts seed into the ground and it grows up and becomes victory!

It doesn't matter whether you are believing for food on the table or for a fleet of airplanes for transportation to go preach the gospel—*El Shaddai* is on the job, and He is not limited. He knows how to deliver. If you will keep on planting the seed of God's Word, *El Shaddai* will bring the harvest of that Word into your life!

A $6 MILLION HARVEST

Everything Kenneth and I have ever believed for has come to pass, but it all started with planting the seed of God's Word in the ground of our heart. The more we plant, the more we reap.

For instance, in 1990 we got behind on our television bills. We were about $6 million in debt! (That was about three months' worth.) After months of not being able to catch up the television bills, it seemed as if we couldn't get out of the situation. We even considered selling the Eagle Mountain property, but the Lord asked Ken, *You could do that this month, but what would you do next month?*

But a time came when we had a turnabout in our hearts. We tried to lay hold of the situation in faith but just had not been able to make the connection. Then all of a sudden, light came! Something happened in the ground—in our hearts. Ken and I took a stand on the Word of God in faith and we received our deliverance. That impossible-looking financial situation took a turn. Within a little more than three months, those bills were paid off! And from that time until the present, we have never been one day behind on a television bill!

But, you know, today we look back at those three months of financial breakthrough, and we don't know how it happened. There was not any single event that brought it about. God just worked and it was done.

That man in the parable also didn't know how his seed was growing. He just knew harvest was coming. Jesus said this is the way God's kingdom operates!

HARVEST TIME

It's harvest time in the kingdom of God. I believe with all my heart we are nearing the last of the last days. Things have sped up in the realm of the spirit. God's Word has increased in the hearts of His people. Things are happening. The kingdom of God is being manifested. God is breaking through into this natural realm as never before.

I'm excited about that! We are learning how the kingdom of God operates, walking in the power of that kingdom. We know what to do and we are doing it. Harvest is inevitable!

Prayer of Consecration

Lord, I thank You for the privilege of being a depository of Your Word. Your words of life will come out of my mouth and accomplish that for which You have sent them.

I apply that Word to every situation I am facing and release my faith to see the kingdom of God manifested in my life. I walk in freedom, life and the dominion of God's kingdom every day of my life! To You, Lord, goes all the glory.

THINK ON THESE THINGS

*It is not the amount of Word you hear
that determines your results. It's how much
Word you hear with revelation or understanding.*

*When light comes, faith is there. Once the light
comes into your spirit, and you walk out
that revelation, it will prevail in your life.*

God has given you and me everything it takes to live by faith.

*No matter how long it takes for your harvest to
come to fruition, you can't give in or quit.*

*The Word of God will grow up to become
anything right and good in your life for
which you have the spiritual courage to stand.*

*When you stand steadfast in faith in a given situation,
God's Word will come to pass and prosper
in the purpose for which He sent it.*

You have been born again to be a depository of God's Word.

PRAYER FOR SALVATION AND BAPTISM IN THE HOLY SPIRIT

Heavenly Father, I come to You in the Name of Jesus. Your Word says, **"Whosoever shall call on the name of the Lord shall be saved"** (Acts 2:21). I am calling on You. I pray and ask Jesus to come into my heart and be Lord over my life, according to Romans 10:9-10. **"If thou shalt confess with thy mouth the Lord Jesus, and shalt believe in thine heart that God hath raised him from the dead, thou shalt be saved. For with the heart man believeth unto righteousness; and with the mouth confession is made unto salvation."** I do that now. I confess that Jesus is Lord, and I believe in my heart that God raised Him from the dead.

I am now reborn! I am a Christian—a child of Almighty God! I am saved! You also said in Your Word, **"If ye then, being evil, know how to give good gifts unto your children: HOW MUCH MORE shall your heavenly Father give the Holy Spirit to them that ask him?"** (Luke 11:13). I'm also asking You to fill me with the Holy Spirit. Holy Spirit, rise up within me as I praise God. I fully expect to speak with other tongues as You give me utterance (Acts 2:4).

Begin to praise God for filling you with the Holy Spirit. Speak those words and syllables you receive—not in your own language, but the language given you by the Holy Spirit. You have to use your own voice. God will not force you to speak. Worship and praise Him in your heavenly language—in other tongues.

Continue with the blessing God has given you and pray in tongues each day.

You are a born-again, Spirit-filled believer. You'll never be the same!

Find a good Word of God preaching church, and become a part of a church family who will love and care for you as you love and care for them.

We need to be connected to each other. It increases our strength in God. It's God's plan for us.

About the Author

Gloria Copeland is an author and minister of the gospel whose teaching ministry is known throughout the world. Believers worldwide know her through Believers' Conventions, Victory Campaigns, magazine articles, teaching tapes and videos, and the daily and Sunday *Believer's Voice of Victory* television broadcast, which she hosts with her husband, Kenneth Copeland. She is known for "Healing School," which she began teaching and hosting in 1979 at KCM meetings. Gloria delivers the Word of God and the keys to victorious Christian living to millions of people every year.

Gloria has written many books, including *God's Will for You, Walk With God, God's Will Is Prosperity, Walk in the Spirit* and *Living Contact.* She has also co-authored several books with her husband, including *Family Promises, Healing Promises* and the best-selling daily devotional, *From Faith to Faith.*

She holds an honorary doctorate from Oral Roberts University. In 1994, Gloria was voted Christian Woman of the Year, an honor conferred on women whose example demonstrates outstanding Christian leadership. Gloria is also the co-founder and vice president of Kenneth Copeland Ministries in Fort Worth, Texas.

Learn more about Kenneth Copeland Ministries
by visiting our website at **www.kcm.org.**

MATERIALS TO HELP YOU RECEIVE YOUR HEALING
BY GLORIA COPELAND

Books

* And Jesus Healed Them All
  God's Prescription for Divine Health
  God's Will for Your Healing
* Harvest of Health

Audiotapes

God Is a Good God
God Wants You Well
Healing School

Videotapes

Healing School: God Wants You Well

OTHER BOOKS AVAILABLE
FROM KENNETH COPELAND MINISTRIES

by Gloria Copeland

* And Jesus Healed Them All
  Are You Ready?
  Build Your Financial Foundation
  Build Yourself an Ark
  Fight On!
  God's Prescription for Divine Health
  God's Success Formula
  God's Will for You
  God's Will for Your Healing
  God's Will Is Prosperity
* God's Will Is the Holy Spirit
* Harvest of Health
  Hidden Treasures
  Living Contact
  Living in Heaven's Blessings Now
* Love—The Secret to Your Success
  No Deposit—No Return
  Pleasing the Father
  Pressing In—It's Worth It All
  Shine On!
  The Power to Live a New Life
  The Unbeatable Spirit of Faith
* Walk in the Spirit
  Walk With God
  Well Worth the Wait

by Kenneth Copeland

* A Ceremony of Marriage
  A Matter of Choice
  Covenant of Blood

Faith and Patience—The Power Twins
* Freedom From Fear
Giving and Receiving
Honor—Walking in Honesty, Truth and Integrity
How to Conquer Strife
How to Discipline Your Flesh
How to Receive Communion
Living at the End of Time—A Time of Supernatural Increase
Love Never Fails
Managing God's Mutual Funds
* Now Are We in Christ Jesus
* Our Covenant With God
* Prayer—Your Foundation for Success
* Prosperity: The Choice Is Yours
Rumors of War
* Sensitivity of Heart
* Six Steps to Excellence in Ministry
* Sorrow Not! Winning Over Grief and Sorrow
* The Decision Is Yours
* The Force of Faith
* The Force of Righteousness
The Image of God in You
The Laws of Prosperity
* The Mercy of God
The Miraculous Realm of God's Love
The Outpouring of the Spirit—The Result of Prayer
* The Power of the Tongue
The Power to Be Forever Free
The Troublemaker
* The Winning Attitude
Turn Your Hurts Into Harvests
* Welcome to the Family
* You Are Healed!
Your Right-Standing With God

Books Co-Authored by Kenneth and Gloria Copeland
Family Promises
Healing Promises
Prosperity Promises
Protection Promises

* From Faith to Faith—A Daily Guide to Victory
From Faith to Faith—A Perpetual Calendar

One Word From God Series
- One Word From God Can Change Your Destiny
- One Word From God Can Change Your Family
- One Word From God Can Change Your Finances
- One Word From God Can Change Your Formula for Success
- One Word From God Can Change Your Health
- One Word From God Can Change Your Nation
- One Word From God Can Change Your Prayer Life
- One Word From God Can Change Your Relationships

Over The Edge—A Youth Devotional
Over the Edge Xtreme Planner for Students—
    Designed for the School Year
Pursuit of His Presence—A Daily Devotional
Pursuit of His Presence—A Perpetual Calendar

*Available in Spanish

WORLD OFFICES
OF KENNETH COPELAND MINISTRIES

For more information about KCM and a free
catalog, please write the office nearest you:

Kenneth Copeland Ministries
Fort Worth, Texas 76192-0001

Kenneth Copeland
Locked Bag 2600
Mansfield Delivery Centre
QUEENSLAND 4122
AUSTRALIA

Kenneth Copeland
Post Office Box 15
BATH
BA1 1GD
ENGLAND U.K.

Kenneth Copeland
Private Bag X 909
FONTAINEBLEAU 2032
REPUBLIC OF SOUTH AFRICA

Kenneth Copeland
Post Office Box 378
Surrey, BC V3T 5B6
CANADA

UKRAINE
L'VIV 290000
Post Office Box 84
Kenneth Copeland Ministries
L'VIV 290000
UKRAINE

WE'RE HERE FOR YOU!

Believer's Voice of Victory Television Broadcast

Join Kenneth and Gloria Copeland and the *Believer's Voice of Victory* broadcasts Monday through Friday and on Sunday each week, and learn how faith in God's Word can take your life from ordinary to extraordinary. This teaching from God's Word is designed to get you where you want to be—*on top!*

You can catch the *Believer's Voice of Victory* broadcast on your local, cable or satellite channels.

*Check your local listings for times and stations in your area.

Believer's Voice of Victory Magazine

Enjoy inspired teaching and encouragement from Kenneth and Gloria Copeland and guest ministers each month in the *Believer's Voice of Victory* magazine. Also included are real-life testimonies of God's miraculous power and divine intervention into the lives of people just like you!

It's more than just a magazine—it's a ministry.

Shout! ...The dynamic magazine just for kids!

Shout! The Voice of Victory for Kids is a Bible-charged, action-packed, bimonthly magazine available FREE to kids everywhere! Featuring *Wichita Slim* and *Commander Kellie and the Superkids*, *Shout!* is filled with colorful adventure comics, challenging games and puzzles, exciting short stories, solve-it-yourself mysteries and much more!!

Stand up, sign up and get ready to *Shout!*

To receive a FREE subscription to *Believer's Voice of Victory,* or to give a child you know a FREE subscription to *Shout!,* write:

Kenneth Copeland Ministries
Fort Worth, Texas 76192-0001
Or call:
1-800-600-7395
(9 a.m.-5 p.m. CT)
Or visit our website at:
www.kcm.org

If you are writing from outside the U.S., please contact the KCM office nearest you. Addresses for all Kenneth Copeland Ministries offices are listed on the previous page.

THE HARRISON HOUSE VISION

Proclaiming the truth and the power
Of the Gospel of Jesus Christ
With excellence;

Challenging Christians to
Live victoriously,
Grow spiritually,
Know God intimately.